Help! I just Became a Dad!

CALEB DARNELL

Sweet Chillies

Sweet Chillies

First Published by Sweet Chillies 2025

ISBN: 978-81-955984-9-6

Table of Contents

Introduction

Ah, fatherhood! You probably didn't exactly sign up for that magical, terrifying, explosive-diaper-filled adventure, but here you are anyway. If you're reading this, you've either just welcomed your tiny overlord into the world or you're pacing up and down the maternity ward passage, chewing up your fingernails and anxiously awaiting the entry of the tiny human who is going to turn your life upside down.

Let me start by saying: *you are not alone.*

And you're also probably not okay—but that's fine. That's *normal.*

Why this book?

I'll never forget the moment I officially became a dad. There I was, overly confident, armed with Google knowledge and YouTube tutorials. I had practiced folding onesies like origami. I had watched countless videos titled, *"Swaddling Like a Pro."* I even downloaded an app that claimed it would "decode baby cries." (Spoiler alert: the app lied.)

The nurse placed my baby in my arms, and she immediately let out a noise that can only be described as an angry goat on a rollercoaster. Panic set in. She was looking at me like, *"So, what's the plan, Dad?"*

My wife, still recovering, gave me that exhausted-yet-amused look, as if to say, *"Good luck, buddy. You're on your own!"*

And that's when it hit me: I had absolutely no clue what I was doing.

None of us do.

Sure, there are books out there (written by people with suspiciously calm babies) or written for moms (which is fine, but we need our own playbook too!). I either didn't understand them or I couldn't relate to them.

Hence, I wrote this book. I wish I'd had something like this when I started, something that didn't make me feel like an idiot, or worse, like I had to be perfect. I wanted a guide that let me laugh at the chaos while actually giving me tools to survive it.

Now, you have that guide in your hands.

Statutory Warning: *This book is not a magic wand, it will not make you a perfect dad.* There is no such thing.

What this book *will* do is help you become the best version of the dad you already are deep down - the one who is clueless but caring, the one who makes silly mistakes but shows up every day.

This book is your survival guide, your playbook, your trusty sidekick. It will help you to

- laugh through the madness,
- learn real, practical dad hacks that actually work,
- avoid rookie mistakes,
- and most importantly, to remind you that you're not in this alone.

I've structured this book like a friendly roadmap through the wild jungle of new fatherhood. Every chapter tackles a *real-world challenge* you will almost definitely face (or already have).

Welcome to the dad club, my friend. No refunds, but unlimited rewards.

Caleb Darnell

CHAPTER 1

Wait… They Let Me Take the Baby Home?!

A Crash Course in Pretending You Know What You're Doing

> *"Having a baby is like suddenly getting a job you never applied for, with no training, and your boss screams at you in gibberish."*
>
> – Anonymous

The 'Oh Crap' Moment

You're standing in the hospital, holding a tiny human burrito wrapped in a hospital blanket. A nurse—who, until now, has been your lifeline—hands you a stack of papers and says, "Alright, you're all set!"

Wait. *What?*

You scan the room, expecting someone to jump out with a "Just kidding! There's no way we're letting *you* be responsible for this fragile, squishy creature."

But no, they really are letting you take this baby home!

At this moment, you may feel a mix of terror, excitement, and the overwhelming realization that you have no idea what you're doing.

> ***Did You Know?***
> *First-time dads experience a 33% increase in stress levels in the first month after bringing the baby home. (Source: Journal of Family Psychology)*

I Have No Idea What I'm Doing!

Let's address the elephant in the room: you have absolutely no clue what you're doing.

The first time you try to change a diaper, it will look like a slapstick comedy scene. The first time you attempt to burp your baby, you'll be convinced you're either going to break them or they'll break you. And feeding? Oh boy. You will learn the hard way that babies have an incredible ability to projectile spit milk with sniper-like precision.

But here's the good news: *you're not alone*. Every first-time dad experiences the same heart-stopping terror of holding something that looks as delicate as a Fabergé egg but screams like a malfunctioning fire alarm.

Excuse Me, Where Is The Baby's User Manual?

The biggest mind trip of becoming a dad is realizing how little preparation the world gives you. If you buy a new TV, it comes with an 80-page instruction manual. If you get a new phone, there are tutorials, FAQs, and customer support numbers.

Your baby? *Nothing*! Just a "good luck" from the hospital staff and a diaper that you'll struggle to figure out which side is the front.

So, like every clueless new parent, you do what seems logical: *you seek advice*. You ask family, friends, and the Internet.

Big mistake.

Every single person you know will suddenly have *expert parenting advice*: your mom, your neighbor, the Uber driver—*everyone*. And guess what? Half of it will contradict the other half.

- "Always pick up the baby when they cry!"
- "Never pick up the baby when they cry!"
- "You should start sleep training at 6 weeks!"
- "Sleep training is a form of baby torture!"
- "Bundle up the baby, babies are fragile and get cold easily."
- "Don't overdress them, or they'll overheat and combust."

At some point, you will find yourself Googling, *"Will my baby die if I use the wrong brand of diaper?"*

Spoiler alert: No, they won't.

Real-Life Anecdote

Steve from California has what you might call "friendly neighbors." The kind who *love* to give unsolicited parenting advice. When Steve's daughter, Madison, was just a week old, he decided to take her for a peaceful stroller walk around the block. Within minutes, he was swarmed like a rookie quarterback in his first NFL game.

First neighbor: "Don't forget to swaddle her tighter! Babies love being wrapped like burritos."

Second neighbor: "Careful, swaddling too tight can cause hip problems."

Third neighbor: "Honestly, skip the swaddle. Skin-to-skin contact is all they need."

Steve stood there, nodding like a bobblehead at a used car lot, utterly overwhelmed. Madison, sensing the rising tension, let out an ear-splitting scream.

One neighbor actually clapped her hands and declared, "See? She agrees with me!"

Steve never took that stroller route again.

Babies Are Easy!

There's always that one person who will tell you, "Babies are easy. They just eat, sleep, and poop."

This is *a lie.*

Yes, they eat, sleep, and poop—but they do these things *at random, unpredictable, and highly inconvenient times.* They will eat when you're trying to sleep, poop when you're trying to eat, and scream when you're trying to have a moment of peace.

Babies also have an incredible ability to sense when you're about to do something important. Need to jump on a work call? BOOM—diaper blowout. Hoping to sneak in a quick nap? LOL—time to wail for no reason. Thinking of spending five whole minutes alone in the bathroom? Good luck! Your baby will demand attention like a tiny dictator.

Welcome to fatherhood. You've got this *(probably).*

> ***Did You Know?***
> *Studies show new parents lose an average of 109 minutes of sleep per night in the first year. That's about 27 full days of lost sleep! (Source: Sleep Foundation)*

How To Pretend You Know What You're Doing

Since you're now a dad, people will assume you have some level of authority. Your partner will look to you for support, friends will ask you for updates, strangers will nod at you like you're part of an elite parenting club.

Here's a pro tip: *Fake it till you make it.*

- Hold the baby with confidence (even if you feel like you're cradling a ticking time bomb).
- Nod wisely when someone gives you advice, then immediately forget it.
- Pretend you understand baby cries (even though they all sound the same).

And when in doubt? Just say "We're taking it day by day." It works every time.

You've Got This!

Look, I won't sugarcoat it—*the first few weeks of fatherhood are absolute chaos.* You will be tired, you will be confused, you will question every decision you make.

But you know what? *You will figure it out.*

One day, without even realizing it, you'll change a diaper in record time. You'll hold your baby like a pro. You'll recognize that a certain cry sound means hunger, and another cry sound means "I just want to mess with you."

And one night—probably at 2:47 a.m.—you'll be rocking your baby to sleep, exhausted but staring at them in complete awe. That's when it hits you: *I may have no idea what I'm doing, but somehow… I'm doing it.*

Check How Are You Doing?

✅ Dad Confidence Checklist

Rate yourself on the following, 1 point for a yes and 0 for a no.

1. I have held my baby without feeling like I'm defusing a bomb.
2. I can successfully feed my baby without wearing half of the milk.
3. I have changed at least one diaper without gagging (or crying).

4. I have nodded and smiled through unsolicited advice without starting a debate.
5. I have accepted that "sleep" is a distant memory.
6. I have learned to carry wipes like they are currency.
7. I have successfully swaddled my baby (or at least tried).
8. I no longer panic when my baby makes weird noises.
9. I have figured out at least one way to soothe my crying baby.
10. I still have a sense of humor about all of this.

Score Yourself:
8-10 Points: You're *basically* a parenting ninja!
5-7 Points: You're surviving—and that's what counts.
0-4 Points: Welcome to the club. No one has it all figured out!

CHAPTER 2

Babies Are Expensive... Can I Return Mine?

Why Your Wallet Will Cry More Than Your Baby

"No one warned me that having a baby would feel like getting financially mugged in broad daylight… daily"

– Anonymous

Congratulations! You've Just Acquired the Most Expensive Thing You'll Ever Own!

Welcome to fatherhood, where your pay check is no longer yours, your credit card now fears for its life, and you find yourself wondering aloud, *"Can I afford to raise this tiny, expensive human without selling a kidney?"*

Before becoming a dad, you probably thought you had a handle on your finances. Maybe you had a budget. Maybe you even saved money. But now? Now you're standing in a baby store, holding a tiny onesie that somehow costs more than your best pair of jeans, wondering how something that small could *possibly* be worth 30 bucks!

My friend, welcome to the *black hole* of baby expenses.

Wait, How Much Does a Baby Cost??

Let's rip the Band-Aid off quickly.

> 💡 ***Did You Know?***
> *The average cost of raising a child in the U.S. from birth to age 18 is a whopping $310,000! Yes, you read that right. So, the annual hit on your bank balance will $17,220 (excluding inflation).*

Now, let's break it down a little so you know *where* all your money is about to disappear:

Expense	Estimated Cost (Per Year)
Diapers & Wipes	$900 – $1,200
Formula/Baby Food	$1,200 – $2,400
Baby Gear (Stroller, Car Seat, etc.)	$2,000 – $3,500
Clothing (Because They Grow Too Fast)	$600 – $1,000
Daycare (The Real Wallet Killer)	$10,000 – $15,000
Medical Expenses	$1,500 – $3,000

Total First-Year Damage? *Easily $15,000 – $20,000.* And that's just the basic stuff.

Real-Life Anecdote

Jake was a first-time dad who thought he could handle a simple baby shopping trip. His wife handed him a list and said, "Just grab a few essentials."

Sounds simple, right?

Cut to Jake, two hours later, standing in the checkout line at a baby store, *clutching a $500 receipt,* wondering what just happened.

Did he buy a diamond-encrusted pacifier? A stroller with built-in wi-fi?

No. He bought:

- A baby bathtub (apparently, the sink was *not* an option).
- A tiny bathrobe (*why?* No one knows).
- A fancy diaper pail that promised to *trap odors (promises are meant to be broken).*
- A nightlight that *projected stars onto the ceiling.*

💡 ***Pro Dad Hack:*** *Stick to the list. Or better yet, send someone who won't impulse-buy a luxury baby robe.*

How to Baby-Proof Your Wallet (Before Your Baby Destroys It)

You can't *avoid* spending money, but you *can* spend it *smarter*. Here's how:

Beware of the 'must-have' baby gear trap. Baby stores are designed to convince you that your child *needs* an $800 stroller with *NASA-level engineering.* But here's the truth:

⃠ You don't need a wipe warmer (*your baby will survive a room-temperature butt wipe*).

⃠ You don't need a high-tech baby monitor with night vision and a built-in lullaby orchestra.

⃠ You don't need a diaper bag that costs more than your monthly rent.

What you do need:

✓ A safe car seat (*legally required*).

✓ A reliable crib (*because sleep is precious*).
✓ A basic stroller (*unless you plan on carrying your baby like a sack of potatoes*).

Everything else? *Optional.*

> 💡 ***Pro Dad Hack:*** *Before buying anything, ask yourself:*
> - *Will my baby actually notice if I don't buy this?*
> - *Can I find a cheaper (but still safe) version?*
> - *Is this something I'll still use in 6 months?*
>
> *If the answer is no to at least two of these, put the item back. Walk away. Your wallet will thank you.*

The Baby Budget Blueprint (A.K.A. How Not to Go Broke)

You can't control how much your baby eats, poops, or demands your attention at 3 a.m. But you *can* control how much you spend.

Here's a simple 3-Step Baby Budget Plan:

Step 1: Set up the "Oh Crap" fund

Babies love surprise expenses. From unexpected doctor visits to emergency diaper runs, you *will* spend money you didn't plan for.

> 💡 ***Pro Dad Hack:*** *Start a 'Baby Emergency Fund' before the baby arrives. Aim for at least $1,000 to cover random, unavoidable baby-related surprises.*

Step 2: Go second-hand where it makes sense

Some baby gear gets used for *a few months* before it's outgrown. Instead of buying brand new, check:

- Facebook Marketplace
- Local parent groups
- Friends and family

🚨 **What NOT to buy used:**

❌ Car seats (*safety first!*)

❌ Cribs with missing parts (*your baby is not a science experiment*)

❌ Bottles & pacifiers (*just… no*)

Step 3: Plan for the Big Expenses Early

- **Daycare:** If you'll need it, start looking NOW. The best places have waitlists longer than your Amazon purchase history.
- **Medical Bills:** If you haven't already, find out what your insurance covers. Hospital bills for childbirth can range from $5,000 to $30,000, depending on your coverage.
- **Future Savings:** Put away $50-$100 per month for future expenses in index funds. Your future self (*and your kid's college fund*) will thank you.

Real-Life Anecdote

Meet *Mike*. A few weeks after his baby was born, he opened the mailbox and nearly passed out on receiving a hospital bill for *$30,000*!

Turns out, he *forgot* to add the baby to his health insurance within the 30-day window (*rookie mistake*).

💡 ***Pro Dad Hack:*** *Check your insurance policy asap.*

CHAPTER 3

Handle with Care: Baby Feels Like a Fragile Package

How to Hold, Carry, and NOT Drop Your Kid

> *"Holding a newborn feels like defusing a bomb—one wrong move, and BOOM (crying explosion)."*
>
> – Anonymous

If you've ever been handed a wriggling baby for the first time and thought, *'What if I drop this priceless potato?'*, you are not alone. According to a study by the Journal of Perinatal Education, nearly *70% of new fathers admitted they were terrified of holding their newborns at first.* (The other 30% were probably lying).

Kath Reas recounts this real-life anecdote on Quora: "When I was newly pregnant with our first child my husband's nephew came to visit with his wife and their new baby. The nephew asked my husband if he would like to hold the baby, and my husband, a long-time bachelor and new to this 'baby' business, looked positively stricken and said, "Thanks, but if I'm going to drop one, it'll be my own!" (He never dropped any of our children)."

This chapter is your survival guide. We'll tackle the basics of baby handling—holding, carrying, swaddling, and of course, keeping the kiddo safe from gravity's evil intentions.

Baby Physics 101 — They *Feel* Fragile, But They're Not Made of Glass

Babies look like they could shatter if you sneeze near them, but the good news is, they're not nearly as fragile as they seem. Nature built them with a few safeguards—like squishy heads that help them during birth and natural reflexes that make them clingy little koalas.

> ***Did You Know?***
> *The soft spot on your baby's head is called the fontanelle, and it's totally normal. It closes up by about 18 months. Until then, think of it as nature's sunroof.*

Quick Rules of Thumb:

- Head and neck support are non-negotiable.
- Keep movements smooth, not jerky.
- Avoid awkward 'limp noodle' handling. Nobody likes being a floppy spaghetti.

The Classic Holds (No Fancy Moves Required)

Alright, let's talk grip. There's no need for ninja moves here. Master these basic holds and you'll feel like a pro.

1. The Cradle Hold

This is the classic. Lay your baby's head in the crook of your elbow, support their back with your forearm, and let their body rest along your arm. Looks fancy. Feels natural.

Bonus? you'll look good in family photos.

💡 ***Pro Dad Hack:*** *Pretend you're holding a warm burrito. Cradle it like you don't want any of the goodness to spill out.*

2. The Shoulder Snuggle

Lift your baby so their head rests on your shoulder. Support their head and neck with one hand and their bottom with the other. Great for soothing and burping. Also great for covering your shirt in unexpected bodily fluids.

3. The Football Hold

Tuck your baby under your arm like you're protecting the winning touchdown. Good for feeding and maneuvering around tight spaces.

🏈 *Fun Fact:* NFL players are not allowed to fumble. Neither are dads.

Swaddling—Because Even Babies Love Burritos

Swaddling looks complicated, like advanced origami, but trust me, it's magic. Swaddling keeps your baby snug, warm, and feeling secure. Plus, it helps with sleep. Studies from the Journal of Pediatrics show *swaddled babies wake less often and sleep longer stretches.*

Translation? Dad gets more sleep. Win-win!

Swaddle Steps:

1. Lay out the blanket in a diamond shape.
2. Fold the top corner down to form a triangle.
3. Place the baby in the centre, with shoulders just below the fold.
4. Gently bring one side of the blanket across the baby and tuck it under.

5. Fold up the bottom corner over the feet.
6. Wrap the other side snugly (but not too tight).

> 💡 ***Pro Dad Hack:*** *Think of wrapping a burrito, not mummifying an ancient king. Snug, not suffocating.*

If all else fails, there are pre-made swaddle sacks with Velcro.

The Art of Calm

Holding your baby isn't just about keeping them physically safe, it's about emotional connection too.

Babies can sense when you're tense. If you're holding them like they're a glass chandelier, they'll feel your anxiety. Breathe, relax your shoulders, and pretend you've done this a thousand times.

"Your calm is contagious. So is your panic."

— Pediatrician Dr. Harvey Karp

Hands Free—The Ultimate Pro Dad Hack

Want to free your hands while still keeping your baby close? Welcome to the world of baby carriers.

There are all kinds: wraps, slings, structured carriers. Find what works for you and wear it with pride.

> ***Did You Know?***
> *A study in Pediatrics journal found that babies who are carried more than three hours a day cry 43% less and bond better with their caregivers.*
> Bonus: Walking around with your baby strapped to you doubles as cardio.

Try This Now! Carry a Watermelon for a Day

Yes, really. Wrap it in a blanket, carry it around, and pretend it's your baby. (Warning: don't try swaddling at the grocery store, people stare). It builds muscle memory and helps you stay cool under pressure.

Bonus points if you manage to cook dinner or send an email one-handed while holding your new "baby."

Closing Thoughts & Key Chapter Takeaways

There's no diploma for baby handling, but here's the thing—you're learning every single day. If you're still feeling nervous, that's normal. Confidence grows with every hold, carry, and burp session.

Here's the good news: Babies are incredibly adaptable. They don't expect perfection—they expect love, warmth, and safety. The more you practice, the more natural it will feel.

Here's a quick chapter recap:

- ☑ **Support the head and neck at all times.**
  Your baby's neck muscles are still on vacation. Give them a hand (literally).
- ☑ **Master a few basic holds.**
  Cradle hold, shoulder snuggle, and football hold will cover most situations.
- ☑ **Practice calm carrying.**
  Your baby feels your emotions. Stay cool and confident.
- ☑ **Swaddle for better sleep.**
  A snug swaddle = more Zzzs for everyone.
- ☑ **Try baby carriers.**
  Boost bonding and enjoy hands-free convenience.

CHAPTER 4

Baby Tech: When Your Crib Has More Features Than Your Car

Surviving the High-Tech Jungle of Modern Baby Gear

> *"They say babies don't come with manuals. Turns out, their gadgets do. 400 pages each."*
>
> — Anonymous

Welcome to the future, Dad. No flying cars yet, but your baby's crib probably has Bluetooth. The diaper pail has Wi-Fi and the bottle warmer is smarter than your college roommate.

I remember standing in the baby aisle, looking at a self-rocking bassinet with built-in white noise, cry detection, and app integration, — basically, a bassinet that would not only rock my baby but also email me if it sensed any crying, farting, or existential threat.

I thought, *wow, this crib is doing more parenting than me.*

> ***Did You Know?***
> *According to a 2024 report from BabyCenter, the baby tech market is now worth over $4.3 billion?*

The Rise of Robo-Parenting

Modern parenting has officially gone full sci-fi. We now have:

- AI-powered baby monitors that analyze your baby's breathing patterns.
- Cribs that rock your baby automatically based on their cry pitch.
- Diapers with moisture sensors that send a notification to your phone. (Because, clearly, your nose wasn't fast enough.)

Real- Life Anecdote

Not kidding! My friend Jake once proudly told me he'd installed a sensor on his baby's onesie. "It tracks her heart rate, skin temperature, and whether she's rolling over," he exclaimed proudly.

Well, his daughter Emma ignored all the tech, found the power cord, and tried to chew it.

Moral? *Baby tech is cool, but it won't replace your arms, ears, or common sense.*

Demystifying Baby Tech

Let's break down some of the most popular baby gadgets, so you don't end up in a panic during a 2 a.m. crying spree.

1. Smart Baby Monitors

They come with night vision, cry detection, temperature readings, and even humidity tracking. Some models let you talk to your baby through your phone—so you can say comforting things like, "Go back to sleep, please, I'm begging you."

> **Pro Dad Hack:** *Try not to obsessively watch the monitor all night. Unless you enjoy mini heart attacks every time your baby sneezes.*

2. Auto-Rocking Bassinets

These are like mini amusement park rides for babies. They sway, vibrate, play white noise, and basically do everything except change diapers. Some models even detect your baby's cry and adjust motion patterns.

Real-Life Anecdote

My buddy Mike set his bassinet to 'Level 5 Turbo Rock' mode, and it jiggled so hard, the cat got motion sickness just watching.

3. Formula Makers

Think of them like Keurigs, but for baby bottles. Add water and formula, press a button, and voilà! Perfect temperature, no clumps, and ready in seconds.

> ***Did You Know?***
> *The Baby Brezza Formula Pro Advanced can prepare a bottle in less than 30 seconds. Faster than you can say, "Please don't wake the baby."*

4. Diaper Sensors

Attach it to the diaper, and it'll ping your phone when things get... swampy.

> **Pro Dad Hack:** *Honestly, your nose is still the most accurate sensor.*

When Tech Takes Over (And When It Shouldn't)

Baby tech is like hot sauce: a little can make things better, too much can burn you alive.

Don't let tech make you a paranoid mess. Watching your baby's heart rate graph for hours will not help you sleep. Neither will checking humidity readings every ten minutes.

A dad named Chris from Ohio once told me he spent three nights refreshing his baby monitor app from bed instead of actually sleeping. "I realized I was basically a zombie with Wi-Fi," he said.

Remember:

- ✅ Tech should *help, not control.*
- ✅ If your device makes you more anxious, *it's okay to turn it off.*
- ✅ Old-school parenting (your *arms, eyes, instincts*) is still *undefeated.*

Real-Life Anecdote

Jake, proud dad of twins, installed a monitor with cry detection. It worked so well, it notified him *every time* one baby cried. Since one baby crying woke the other, the monitor buzzed like an airport runway light show.

He finally turned it off after 48 hours of non-stop pinging.

Lesson? *Sometimes silence really is golden.*

Laughing Through the Glitches

The best way to handle baby tech glitches? Laugh at them. Your gadgets will beep randomly, flash lights like a disco, and sometimes act like they need tech support themselves.

> *"Technology is great... when it works."*
>
> — Every Parent Ever

Here's the truth: you're already doing great. Tech or no tech, your baby's favorite feature is *you.* Not your smart bottle warmer.

Try This Now!

Unplug one "essential" baby gadget for a full day. Go ahead. See if you survive. (Spoiler: You absolutely will).

I tried this myself. I turned off our smart monitor for one day. Was I a little twitchy at first? Sure. But something magical happened. I started trusting my ears. I noticed my daughter's sleepy grumbles without a screen telling me. I felt like… an actual parent!

Tech is great, but your baby's first smile doesn't need a firmware update.

Try This Now!

Okay, let's do a quick self-check. Rate yourself from 1 to 10 for each statement below:

Statement	***Score (1–10)***
I can set up the baby monitor without calling tech support.	
I know how to warm a bottle without a smart warmer.	
I resist the urge to check the baby app every five minutes.	
I remember to pack spare batteries for gadgets.	
I use tech to help, not to stress.	
I can still change a diaper in the dark without a motion sensor.	
I know how to open and close a baby stroller.	
I've successfully turned off a baby gadget without causing a household crisis.	

Scoring:

- ***0–30:*** *Tech Overload Alert — Take a breath. Remember, you're the parent, not the robot.*
- ***31–60:*** *Balanced Tech Dad — Nice! Using tech as a tool, not a crutch.*
- ***61–80:*** *Jedi Tech Master — You're in control of the gear, and the force is strong with you.*

Closing Thoughts & Key Chapter Takeaways

Let's get honest for a second: *our parents raised us with zero smart gadgets. Zero*! Their fanciest tech was probably a rubber pacifier and a wind-up mobile.

And guess what? We survived. Mostly.

Remember:

- ☑ Baby tech is cool, but not essential.
- ☑ Use tech to help, not to panic.
- ☑ Unplug occasionally—you'll survive (and thrive).
- ☑ Laugh at tech fails. Seriously, they make great stories.
- ☑ Remember: you're the smartest gadget in the nursery.

CHAPTER 5

The In-Law Invasion

Navigating Family Advice Without Losing Your Sanity (or Sleep)

"Everyone becomes a parenting expert the moment your baby arrives."

– Unknown

Guess Who's Coming to Stay (Forever?)

The moment you become a parent, your doorbell starts working overtime. Except it's not delivering pizza or baby wipes — it's summoning an army of well-meaning relatives armed with casseroles, unsolicited advice, and stories that start with, *"Back in my day…"*

And leading this battalion? Your in-laws.

Now, let's get something straight: They love your baby. They probably even like you — at least most of the time. But they also love giving advice. Lots of it. Non-stop!

Congratulations, Dad. You're not just raising a baby anymore. You're also learning how to parent… your in-laws.

The Well-Meaning (But Relentless) Experts

The thing about family, especially in-laws, is that they've been waiting for this moment. The moment they can transfer their entire vault of parenting wisdom to you, whether you asked or not.

As comedian Jerry Seinfeld once said, *"There's no such thing as fun for the whole family."*

> 💡 ***Did You Know?***
> *A 2021 survey by BabyCenter found that 65% of new parents feel overwhelmed by family advice in the first three months of parenting.*

Let's meet the typical family 'experts' you'll encounter:

- The Old-School Grandma: "We used *whiskey on the gums*, and look how great your wife turned out!"
- The Competitive Aunt: "My Jeremy walked at eight months. *Have you started baby yoga yet?*"
- The Passive-Aggressive Grandpa: "Oh, you're using disposable diapers? *Interesting…*"

Real-Life Anecdote

Take Bob, a first-time dad from Ohio. Bob's in-laws decided to 'help' during the first week home from the hospital. On Day Two, Bob found himself in a heated debate with his mother-in-law about sterilizing bottles. She insisted boiling them for *exactly* 22 minutes was the only way to ensure 'baby-safe' cleanliness.

Bob, holding the instructions that clearly said 5 minutes, smiled and asked, "Are we sterilizing the bottle or launching it into orbit?"

The mother-in-law didn't laugh.

Moral of the story? *Keep your humor handy, and keep it to yourself only. Your in-laws are not fooling around. The wife (and new mom) isn't going to be too pleased either.*

Setting Boundaries Without Starting World War III

Boundaries are tricky, you want to protect your sanity without offending anyone. Here's the golden rule to deal with unsolicited advice: *firm, but polite.*

Try these three polite, pre-planned responses

- "We're following the doctor's orders on this one — keeps us out of jail!"
- "I know you raised a great kid, and I'm just trying not to mess that up!"
- "We're testing new strategies. It's like beta parenting!"

Write them down. Now practice them in the mirror. Score your comfort level from 1 (awkward turtle) to 10 (dad ninja).

When Family Visits Turn Into Full-Time Occupations

At some point, family visits stop feeling like quick hellos and start feeling like unpaid internships at Camp Baby.

Aunt Linda is folding your laundry (wrong). Uncle Joe is telling you how he never needed baby monitors in his day (great). And your in-laws have officially adopted your living room as their office.

Pro Dad Hack: *Turn family into actual support.*

1. ***Ask for help by delegating:***
   "Could you hold the baby while I take a shower?" Translation: I trust you and need five minutes of alone time.
2. ***Set clear end times:*** *"We have a baby class at 4 p.m." Boundaries = Exit Cards.*
3. ***Praise participation (especially on the activities that you actually want participation):***
   "You rock at burping him!" Everyone loves to feel helpful.

Real-Life Anecdote

Mike from Boston learned this lesson the hard way. His in-laws announced that they were staying for "a few days", which turned into a fortnight. One night, disaster struck: diaper explosion at 2 a.m. The in-laws were awake in the next room.

Instead of suffering solo, Mike asked for help. His mother-in-law, delighted for the chance to demonstrate her swaddling superiority, swooped in like a pro. Ten minutes later, clean sheets, clean baby, and Mike back in bed.

Lesson? *Delegate like your sanity depends on it — because it does.*

Did You Know?

A study by the University of Michigan found that 46% of new parents feel judged by their families over parenting choices. (Source: University of Michigan Health Lab, 2019)

When the Advice Turns to Criticism (and You're About to Lose It)

Let's be honest. Sometimes, family advice stops being helpful and starts sounding like, well… a roast.

"You're holding him wrong."

"She looks cold."

"Why is he crying? You're not feeding him enough."

💡 ***Pro Dad Hack:*** *Use the powerful* ***Compliment Sandwich.***

Serve your feedback like this:

- ***Compliment:*** *"I appreciate your experience."*
- ***Boundary:*** *"But we're comfortable with this method."*
- ***Compliment:*** *"Your support means a lot to us."*

It feels a little cheesy, sure. But it works.

Turning Tension into Teamwork

Surprise: your in-laws actually *want* to be helpful — they just don't always know how. The trick is to channel that energy constructively.

Action Plan:

- Identify Their Superpowers: Is your father-in-law great with DIY? Put him on crib-assembly duty.
- Create a Routine: Schedule visits during the baby's awake time to avoid nap disruption.
- Express Gratitude: Even a simple "We couldn't do this without you" goes a long way.

Try This Now!

Rate your current in-law management strategy from 1–10.

1 = They're running the house.

10 = You've got this down to a fine art.

Write down two things that are working well, and one thing you'd like to improve.

A Note on Sleep and Sanity

Remember: sleep deprivation turns molehills into mountains. A comment that normally rolls off your back can feel like a personal attack at 3 a.m.

Before responding, take a deep breath. Ask yourself: *Is this exhaustion talking? Or is it genuinely over the line?*

If it's the latter, revisit your polite, pre-planned responses. If it's the former, sneak in a nap. Everything feels less apocalyptic after 45 minutes of shuteye.

> 💡 ***Pro Dad Hack:*** *Check your mood first. If it's irritable or bad, just shut up.*

Dad's Quick Emergency Reference: Handling the In-Law Invasion

Scenario	Dad Move
Unsolicited advice overload	Use firmness+ polite deflection
Endless visit dragging on	Set clear end times ("We have baby class at 4!")
Passive-aggressive comments	Deploy the Compliment Sandwich
Helpful in-laws actually being helpful	Express gratitude + assign more tasks

Key Chapter Takeaways

In-laws mean well, even if it feels like they're auditioning for *Parenting Idol.* Turn "helpful" visits into actual help by assigning tasks. Use the Compliment Sandwich and state boundaries politely, very politely.

And always check your mood when receiving advice. If you are in a bad mood, just shut up. Also careful with the humor please because your in-laws may not get it. Instead, you could be putting yourself in the danger zone with the wifey.

~

CHAPTER 6

Google is Not Your Pediatrician

Surviving Baby Health Scares Without Losing Your Mind.

"Google is like that friend who either reassures you or convinces you you're dying of something rare."

— Anonymous

It's 2:37 a.m. You're bleary-eyed, wearing a stained T-shirt that once resembled your favorite, and holding a crying baby who is making noises somewhere between a tea kettle and a car alarm.

Out of pure desperation, you type into Google: "Baby red rash weird triangle pattern HELP."

And boom — *1.2 million results!* The first one suggests your child is fine. The second one says it could be life-threatening. The third one recommends an herbal tea from the mountains of Tibet.

What to do??? PANIC!

Here's the thing about newborns: they come with zero manuals but 100% performance anxiety for parents.

Did You Know?
According to a study by Pew Research Center, 80% of parents admit to googling their child's symptoms before calling a doctor. So, you're in good (nervous) company!

Common first-time dad questions googled at 3 a.m.:

- "Is my baby's poop supposed to be green?"
- "Why does my baby grunt while sleeping?"
- "How loud is too loud for a baby fart?"
- "Baby snorts like a piglet—is this normal?"

In most cases, the answer is: *yes, it's normal. Weird, but normal.* Babies are noisy, gassy, hiccupping little humans, and unless they're running a high fever or showing real distress, they're probably just fine.

Pro Dad Hack:
Before you google, ask yourself: Is the baby eating? Breathing? Pooping? If yes to all three, chances are, you can stop panicking.

Did You Know?
Babies sneeze up to four times more frequently than adults — not because they're sick, but because it's how they clear their little nasal passages. Totally normal. (Source: American Academy of Pediatrics)

Real-Life Anecdote

Zach swore he heard the baby breathing weird at 3 a.m. one night. He nudged his wife awake, full-on panic mode.

"Babe! Is he wheezing? Should we call someone? Google says it could be anything from a blocked nose to—"

His wife calmly got up, walked over to the bassinet, picked up their baby boy, and smiled. "He's snoring," she said. "Just like you!"

'Is This Normal?' — When to Freak Out (and When Not To)

Every new dad has this moment: You're holding your baby, they make a strange noise, and suddenly, Google becomes your frantic best friend.

But here's the truth—babies make a lot of weird sounds and movements that are completely normal.

Totally *Normal* Things That Will Scare You:

- Baby sneezes (yes, a lot),
- Hiccups (all the time!).
- Twitchy arms and legs.
- Poop that changes colour like a mood ring.

Real-Life Anecdote

Kevin, a first-time dad from Ohio, discovered that his baby had developed a tiny red bump on her leg. Harmless, right? Well, Kevin googled it.

First search result: "Normal baby rash."

Second search result: "Rare flesh-eating bacteria."

Kevin panicked, woke up his wife, and demanded an emergency room visit.

Diagnosis? Mosquito bite.

The bill? $300 copay.

The lesson? *Kevin now keeps his phone across the room at night.*

Baby Health Myths

There's a lot of old-school advice out there. Let's clear the air:

Myth	Reality
"Cold weather causes colds."	Nope. Viruses do. Bundle up, but don't panic over chilly air.
"Green poop means infection."	Not necessarily. Diet changes can do this too!
"If the baby hiccups, something's wrong."	False. Baby hiccups are very common and harmless.
"Teething causes fever."	Teething can cause fussiness, but high fever likely means something else. Call your doc.

Did You Know?
Babies get an average of 8–10 colds in their first year. Stock up on tissues — and patience!

When To Actually Call the Pediatrician

Look, you're not expected to be a doctor (unless you actually are, in which case — lucky you!). But you *are* expected to know the basics.

Red Flags Worth a Call:

- Fever over 100.4°F (for babies under 3 months).
- Trouble breathing (more than the usual grunting noises).
- Persistent vomiting or diarrhea.
- Unusual lethargy (sleeping *way* more than usual).
- Rash that spreads quickly or looks infected.
- Poor feeding (refusing to eat).
- Excessive crying that doesn't stop after all the usual checks.

If you're not sure, trust your gut. Call your pediatrician instead of falling down a 3 a.m. Remember: *Google is not your pediatrician.*

💡 ***Pro Dad Hack:*** *Save your pediatrician's number in your phone under 'Lifesaver 🚑'. Trust me, you'll be too panicked to search for it later.*

The Art of Staying Calm (Even When You're Not)

Real-Life Anecdote

Jessica and *Mike*, new parents from Texas, once spent an entire Sunday convinced their baby's belly button stump had fallen off 'too soon'. They took turns googling 'belly button emergency'. Mike even built a tiny bandage fort around it with gauze and tape.

Verdict from their doctor? *Totally normal.* Umbilical stumps usually fall off within 1–3 weeks.

First-Aid 101 (Without Freaking Out)

There's a fine balance between being prepared and turning your home into a mini hospital. You don't need a defibrillator in the nursery, but having basics on hand is smart.

Dad's Basic Baby First-Aid Kit:

- Digital thermometer.
- Nasal aspirator (aka the snot-sucker).
- Baby-friendly fever medication (as per doctor's advice).
- Band-aids.
- Saline drops.
- Gauze and baby-safe antiseptic.

Note: Keep this kit somewhere obvious — not buried under the mountain of diaper boxes.

Try This Now!

1. *Time how long it takes you to find your pediatrician's number, paediatric first-aid kit, and car keys for emergency visits. If it's longer than 60 seconds, reorganize your emergency game!*

2. *Practice using the nasal aspirator before you actually need it. Trust me, it's less gross when you're not in a panic.*

How to Co-Pilot Health Decisions With Your Partner

When the baby coughs, you and your partner may have *very* different reactions:

- You: "It's probably just a dry throat."
- Your partner: "Call the ambulance. NOW!"

This is normal. The best thing you can do is:

- Stay calm (externally, at least).
- Validate your partner's concerns.
- Look up reliable sources *together.*
- Agree on a "panic protocol" in advance: *When do we call the doctor? What symptoms are we watching for?*

💡 ***Pro Dad Hack:*** *Schedule a "health game plan" talk during nap time — not at 3 a.m. when you're both exhausted.*

Closing Thoughts

Remember, Google cannot replace your gut instinct or pediatrician. Whenever you notice something weird or out of the ordinary for your baby, step away from Google unless you love panicking. Instead keep calm and ask, is this normal or is this something you need to consult a pediatrician? Know the red flags that deserve a real doctor's opinion. Keep the doc's number handy and prep your first-aid kit before you need it. Very important, always communicate with your partner — you're a team!

Quick Pit Stop, Dad!

Got 60 Seconds? You Can Help Another Clueless Dad Survive

"The best thing you can do for another new dad?
Tell him he's not crazy."

Would you help clueless, anxious, and overwhelmed new fathers navigate the chaos of parenthood without losing their minds *(or their sense of humor)?*

My mission is to make this topic easy and fun for first-time dads.

But to reach more people, I need your help.

Most people choose books based on reviews. So, I'm asking you to help a fellow dad by leaving a quick review on Amazon.

It costs nothing, takes less than a minute, but it could completely transform someone's fatherhood journey.

Your review could help:

- One more dad avoid Googling "Is it normal if my baby sounds like a goose?"
- One more exhausted parent find comfort in the chaos.
- One more guy feel seen, not scolded.

Simply click the link below or scan the QR code to share your review and make a big difference in someone's life.
https://www.amazon.com/review/review-your-purchases/?asin=BOOKASIN

If you love helping others, you're my kind of person.
Thank you from the bottom of my heart!

Caleb Darnell

CHAPTER 7

The New 24/7 Job You Can't Quit

Balancing Work, Diapers, and the 3 Hours of Sleep You'll Get

"Work-life balance? More like work-life-baby chaos."

– Anonymous

The Ultimate Full-Time, Overtime, No-Time-Off Job

Welcome! You are now the proud employee of *Baby Inc.*, a company with zero benefits, no paid time off, and a boss who screams at you in the middle of the night for reasons you don't understand.

The job description?

- Night shift required.
- Ability to function on no sleep preferred.
- Must endure random, high-volume tantrums.
- Salary: LOL!

The worst part? *You can't quit!*

Balancing work and a newborn is like trying to juggle flaming swords while blindfolded. Your boss (baby) demands 24/7 attention. Your other boss (work) expects you to function like a human being. And you? You just want five minutes to shower without being interrupted by crying or an urgent email.

So, how do you survive this madness? Let's dive in.

'Work-Life Balance?' HA! Good One

Before you had a baby, you thought you understood 'work-life balance'. Maybe you even took lunch breaks, went to the gym, or had hobbies (*RIP to those*). But now?

Your coffee is cold before you get a sip. Your inbox is exploding. You just realized you've been wearing the same socks for three days.

Real-Life Anecdote

Meet Brian, a first-time dad who thought he could handle a simple work-from-home meeting while watching his newborn. He had a big client call at 10 a.m. His plan? Hold the baby, keep calm, and look professional on camera.

The baby threw up on his shirt exactly 12 seconds before the call started. While introducing himself, Brian forgot his own job title. Halfway through, his baby let out a nuclear-level diaper explosion, making a sound so aggressive that the entire Zoom call went silent.

Moral of the story? *Never trust a baby to stay quiet during an important meeting.*

Mastering the Art of the Work-Dad Balance

You can't stop the chaos, but you *can* learn how to manage it. Here's how:

1. Have "The Talk" (No, not that one) with your boss

If you have a supportive boss, they'll understand that your life is currently an unpredictable mess. If you have a terrible boss, well… you'll need some strategic survival skills.

- **Be honest but strategic** – No need to say "My baby just screamed for three straight hours, and I haven't slept since Tuesday." Instead, try "Hey, I may *need some flexibility* while I adjust to this new routine."
- **Be aware** – If you're working remotely, *mute your mic before your baby starts its daily tantrum symphony.*
- **Use 'The Baby Excuse' wisely** – Got a pointless meeting? Announce "Sorry, baby emergency!" (No one can argue with that).

Real-Life Anecdote

Kevin, a new dad, quickly realized that his baby was the *ultimate get-out-of-meeting-free card.* One day, his boss asked him to join a 3-hour strategy meeting (a.k.a. corporate torture). Thinking fast, Kevin picked up his baby, held him up to the camera, and said, "Oh no! Diaper disaster! Gotta go!"

His boss, clearly uncomfortable, waved him off the call immediately. Kevin spent the next three hours napping.

Moral of the story? *Your baby can be an inconvenience or your secret weapon. Choose wisely.*

2. The art of the strategic nap

If sleep was scarce before, it's now an endangered species.

Your baby does not care that you have work in the morning. They will scream at 3 a.m. You have two choices: fight it, or nap strategically.

Use 'Baby Sleep Alignment': When the baby naps, *you nap*. Doesn't matter where and how, it can be the chair, couch, floor, or even standing. Grab any opportunity that comes your way. Even *12 minutes* of shut-eye can prevent a full mental meltdown.

And don't start scrolling reels on your mobile for a second, that's a trap.

> ***Did You Know?***
> *Research indicates that even brief naps, lasting five to fifteen minutes, enhance mood, short-term memory, alertness, and response time.*

3. Work smarter, not harder

You're exhausted, overwhelmed, and somehow still expected to be a functional adult. The trick? *Cheat the system.*

Dad Productivity Hacks:

1. **Batch tasks like a pro** – Do baby-related chores *all at once* (*diaper changes, bottle prep, etc.*) so you don't feel like you're in a constant loop.
2. **Embrace the "good enough" mentality** – Your work doesn't have to be *perfect*—it just has to be *done.*
3. **Use the "Sleeping Baby Deadline"** – If the baby is napping, you have exactly *45 minutes to be the most productive human alive.*

Try This Now!

Check how you are doing: Work-Life-Baby Survival Checklist. For every statement, give yourself 1 point if you say yes, otherwise 0.

- *I have warned my boss that I am now running on 3 hours of sleep.*
- *I have figured out how to mute myself on Zoom faster than a fighter pilot.*
- *I have perfected the "baby excuse" to escape unnecessary work meetings.*
- *I have accepted that my productivity level is now 'do what I can before baby wakes up'.*

- *I have napped in at least one unusual location (desk, car, laundry room).*

*If you scored **3/5 or higher**, congratulations—you are officially a functioning work-dad.*

Key Chapter Takeaways

Welcome to the 24x7 job, where you will actually need to shell out money from your pocket and work for a screaming boss. Work life balance, what's that, huh?

Remember:

- Have the talk with your boss (the office one).
- Use the 'baby excuse' wisely.
- Nap strategically.
- Align your sleep with that of the baby.
- Do whatever you can before your baby wakes up.
- Practice muting your Zoom during meetings so that it becomes second nature.

CHAPTER 8

The Walking Dad: Surviving on No Sleep

How to Function on 2 Hours of Sleep and 6 Cups of Coffee

> *"Sleep when the baby sleeps? LOL. Sure. Right after I finish these 57 chores."*
>
> — Every New Parent Ever

Welcome to the Zombie Club. You've unlocked the bonus level of parenthood: *Sleep Deprivation Mode.*

Here's the kicker—babies do not care about your circadian rhythm. Your baby operates on a 24/7 schedule that appears to have been written by a committee of caffeinated raccoons.

You'll soon find yourself negotiating with higher powers for just two uninterrupted hours. *(Spoiler alert: The negotiations will fail).*

Did You Know?

- *New parents lose around 350 hours of sleep in the first year (That's basically like losing 50 full nights of sleep!)*
- *Studies show that chronic sleep deprivation can make you as cognitively impaired as being legally drunk (so yes, you are basically emailing your boss while mentally intoxicated).*
- *The average working parent spends 50% of their time thinking about sleep (and the other 50% trying to get some).*

Understanding Your New Sleep-Deprived Reality

If you thought pulling an all-nighter in college was rough, think of this as the *Director's Cut* of exhaustion. Except this time, there's no final exam, just endless pop quizzes at 2 a.m.

New dads often enter this phase armed with a dangerous weapon: *false optimism.*

"How bad could it be? I'll sleep when the baby sleeps!"

LOL! When the baby sleeps, you'll be catching up on dishes, laundry, replying to texts that have been ignored for weeks, and trying to remember what your own name is.

Tricks to Maximize Sleep

1. Nap opportunistically

Think like a cat. Sleep whenever the opportunity arises. Yes, even if it's a 12-minute power nap in the laundry room while the dryer hums soothing lullabies.

2. Lower the bar
Forget about eight hours. Aim for *micro-naps* and you'll feel like a champion.

> ***Did You Know?***
> *Short naps of 10-20 minutes can significantly improve alertness and performance, according to Harvard Medical School.*

3. Coffee: your legal stimulant
But remember, coffee is your friend, not your life support system. Overdo it, and you'll be wide awake *while* exhausted, which is like putting your brain in airplane mode.

Real-Life Anecdote
Dan, a new dad from Ohio, swears by 'micro-naps'. One day, Dan dozed off while tying his shoelaces. His wife found him snoring softly, bent over, shoelace in one hand, baby monitor in the other. Surprisingly, Dan woke up feeling mildly refreshed and finished the knot like a pro.

> ***Pro Dad Hack:*** *So you've slept for two hours, and your brain feels like scrambled eggs. How do you look functional?*
> *A brisk splash of cold water is your new best friend.*

Taking Shifts with Your Partner (Teamwork = Survival)

This is not a solo mission. Survival depends on good shift work.

Tips for Tag-Team Parenting:

- Divide the night into "shifts" (e.g., 9 p.m.–2 a.m., 2 a.m.–7 a.m.).
- Respect the sacred nap zone of your partner.
- Do *not* play the *'Who's more exhausted?'* game. Nobody wins.

> ***Pro Dad Hack:*** *Get rid of your phone when you are you are trying to get a shut eye because your phone will tempt you: 'Scroll me, Scroll me!'.*

How to Sleep Train Your Baby (Without Losing Your Mind)

What Is Sleep Training?

Sleep training is the process of helping your baby learn *how to fall asleep on their own—without rocking, feeding, or constant soothing.* It also helps them learn to go back to sleep during nighttime wake-ups. However, it doesn't mean letting your baby cry endlessly or skipping night feeds. Sleep training can be gentle and flexible, depending on what feels right for you.

Most doctors say you can begin around 4 to 6 months of age. At this point, babies can usually sleep longer stretches without needing to eat, and they're ready to learn independent sleep skills.

Popular Sleep Training Methods

You can choose the method that suits your baby and your parenting style:

1. Cry It Out (CIO)

Put baby to bed awake and don't return until morning (unless for feeding). It sounds tough, but many babies adjust in a few nights. It requires consistency.

2. Ferber Method (Check & Console)

Let baby cry for short intervals, *increasing the time* before you check on them. Offer quick comfort, but avoid picking them up. Over time, your baby learns to settle without needing you.

3. Chair Method

Sit next to the crib until baby sleeps, then *slowly move the chair farther away each night* until you're out of the room. It takes longer and may involve some crying when they notice you're gone.

4. Bedtime Fading

Shift bedtime based on when your baby naturally feels tired. If they cry a lot at bedtime, try putting them down later, then *gradually move it earlier over a few nights.* It adjusts their sleep cycle slowly.

5. Pick Up, Put Down

Put the baby down awake. If they cry, wait briefly, then pick them up to soothe. Once calm, place them back in the crib. Repeat until they fall asleep. This can take time and patience.

Tips for Success

- **Create a bedtime routine:** A 30–45 minutes wind-down with bath, books, and cuddles helps the baby know sleep is coming.
- **Time it right:** Don't start during big changes like travel or illness.
- **Watch baby's signals:** Yawning, eye rubbing, fussiness = bedtime. Don't wait too long—overtired babies sleep worse.
- **Put the baby down awake:** This teaches them how to fall asleep on their own.
- **Don't rush in:** Babies often make noises between sleep cycles. Give them a minute to settle.

Sleep-Training Myths vs. Reality

Sleep training sounds like a magic potion. In reality, it's more like a confusing IKEA manual written in hieroglyphics.

Myth #1: Sleep training works overnight.

Reality: It might take days, or weeks. Or longer. Some babies simply laugh in the face of your schedule.

Myth #2: All babies respond to the same method.

Reality: Your baby is not a robot. What worked for your friend's kid might not work for yours. Keep doing trial and error till you find out what works best for your baby.

Myth #3: Letting them cry for a few minutes is cruel.

Reality: Brief, supervised crying is safe and part of many sleep training methods. Just ensure you and your partner are on the same page.

What Is All the Noise About?

Turns out, your baby doesn't need complete silence to sleep—what they really miss is noise. Not the "dad snoring on the couch" kind, but soft, steady white noise that sounds suspiciously like a vacuum cleaner on a coffee break. Why? Because the womb is not exactly a Zen Garden—it's more like a whooshing, gurgling sound machine.

> **_Did You Know?_**
> *According to a study published in Archives of Disease in Childhood, 80% of newborns fell asleep within five minutes of hearing white noise, compared to just 25% without it.*

Creating white noise for your baby is easier than you might think—and you don't need a PhD in sound engineering or a spaceship console. Here are simple, parent-friendly ways to create white noise at home:

1. Use a white noise machine

- These are designed specifically to mimic soothing sounds like rainfall, ocean waves, or static.
- Look for one that has a continuous play mode (not on a timer) and adjustable volume.
- Safe volume: keep it under 50 decibels (about the level of a running shower) and place it at least 7 feet away from the crib.

2. Try a White Noise App

Free or paid apps are available for both Android and iOS. Some popular ones:

- *Sound Sleeper*
- *Baby Sleep Sounds*
- *Hatch*

3. Household hack: Use what you've got

- Fan – A simple table fan or ceiling fan (just for the sound, not blowing directly on baby).
- Hair Dryer (on a safe surface, away from baby—short bursts only).
- Vacuum Cleaner – Surprisingly effective! Record the sound and play it on loop (unless you want clean floors daily).

4. YouTube & Streaming Platforms

- Search "baby white noise" on YouTube, Spotify, or Amazon Music.
- Many offer 10-hour loops so you don't have to restart it at 2 a.m.

⚠ Safety Tips

- Keep devices away from the crib and out of baby's reach.
- Avoid high volumes—white noise should be a gentle hum, not a rock concert.
- Turn it off gradually once your baby starts to sleep better without it (usually around 1 year).

Try This Now!

Track your daily sleep

Day	*Hours Slept (Total)*	*Naps Taken*	*Energy Level (1-10)*	*Notes*
1				
2				
...				

What small changes can you make to your daily routine to snag an extra 15–20 minutes of rest? Jot them down.

Key Chapter Takeaways

- Be opportunistic: Power nap like your sanity depends on it (because it does).
- Keep healthy snacks nearby to fight fatigue.
- Try white noise for baby (and maybe yourself).
- Sleep train your baby.
- Limit caffeine after 2 p.m. to avoid the jittery-zombie state.
- Drink water between coffee cups (Coffee isn't hydration).

- Partner teamwork is essential — take turns on night duty!
- Track your progress to see improvements (even tiny ones).
- Celebrate small victories (like a 2-hour stretch of sleep).

~

CHAPTER 9

Milk Happens: Feeding Your Baby Without Losing Your Mind (or Shirt)

Navigating Bottles, Breasts, and Midnight Hunger Games

> *"Breast milk: the only food that comes in environmentally friendly packaging and is served at exactly body temperature. Can't get that at Starbucks."*
>
> — Anonymous

Alright, Dad. Let's talk about one of the most basic (yet totally confusing) parts of keeping a tiny human alive: feeding them.

You'd think feeding a baby would be simple. They're small, they only drink milk, how hard can this be? Ha.

The moment you step into the baby-feeding universe, it feels like you've stumbled into an ancient debate club where everyone has strong opinions and nobody agrees on anything. Breastfeeding? Formula? Pumping? Bottle or breast? Organic formula imported from a remote village in Switzerland? (Yes, that's a thing.)

Good news: We're going to untangle this, keep you laughing, and save your shirt from milk explosions.

The Feeding Options (a.k.a. The Menu at Baby's Diner)

1. **Breastfeeding:**
   This is the gold standard according to many experts. It's free, always warm, and packed with nutrients. But it also means mom does most of the heavy lifting (or should we say, latching?).

2. **Pumping:**
   This is mom expressing milk with a pump, so you can bottle-feed. It gives you a chance to get involved in feeding time, which is both amazing and slightly terrifying when your baby stares at you like, "Are you sure you know what you're doing?"

3. **Formula:**
   Well, it's convenient. Though it's a little tricky to trust something that's marketed so heavily.

Did You Know?
According to the CDC, around 60% of U.S. moms do not breastfeed exclusively for the first six months.

Note: Leading health authorities consider breastfeeding the optimal choice for mothers and their infants. They advise feeding infants solely on breast milk for the first six months, then keeping it a central part of the child's diet until at least one year—and ideally through age two. Babies who nurse typically deal with fewer illnesses and hospital stays than those given formula. Nursing transfers antibodies and other protective compounds from mother to child, giving the baby's immune system a valuable head start.

Real-Life Anecdote

Kevin, a first-time dad from Ohio, was in charge of bottle feeding while his wife got some well-deserved rest. He proudly filled the bottle, warmed it to a cozy temperature, tested it on his wrist like a pro, and sat down to feed his daughter.

Two seconds into the feed, the cap popped off, and a warm milk geyser shot straight up his shirt. His daughter blinked twice, let out a delighted giggle, and proceeded to sneeze milky mist all over his face.

Lesson? *Always double-check the bottle cap and make sure it's tightened.*

Feeding Frequency?

All the time! If it feels like you're feeding this baby every 17 minutes, that's because… you are.

Newborns typically feed every 2–3 hours, day and night. Yes, *even at 3:47 a.m.,* when your brain is foggier than a Sherlock Holmes mystery.

> 💡 ***Pro Dad Hack:*** *Use an app or even a sticky note to track feedings. Your sleep-deprived brain will not remember if you last fed the baby an hour ago or last Tuesday.*

The Bottle Battle: Picking the Right Gear

Here's a secret: babies have preferences. And they don't care that you bought a fancy bottle set with great Amazon reviews.

Some like wide-neck bottles, some like angled ones, some like slow-flow nipples, and some refuse them all like they're fine-dining critics at a greasy diner.

Be patient and keep experimenting till you get it right.

💡 ***Pro Dad Hack:** Start with a variety pack. It's like speed dating, but for bottles.*

Handling Hunger Cues Like a Pro

Your baby has a secret language of hunger signs before they go full siren mode (a.k.a. screaming). Catch them early, and you'll save yourself from the angry baby noises.

- **Rooting:** Baby turns head and opens mouth like a baby shark.
- **Fists to mouth:** Baby is trying to make a DIY snack.
- **Lip-smacking:** Self-explanatory.
- **Whimpering:** Early warning system!

Try This Now!
Practice spotting these signs during awake times.

Myth-Busting: Feeding Edition

🚫 **Myth 1:** Microwaving bottles is okay.

Truth: Please don't. Microwaves heat unevenly and can create dangerous hot spots. Use warm water or a bottle warmer.

🚫 **Myth 2:** If baby cries, they're always hungry.

Truth: Sometimes they just need comfort, a diaper change, or they're practicing for their future as a soprano.

💡 ***Pro Dad Hack:** Pre-fill bottles and pre-measure formula before you go to bed. That way, when you're half-asleep and questioning your life choices at 2:00 a.m., you won't accidentally pour formula into your coffee mug.*

Burping: Yes, It's a Thing

Don't skip the burp. After feeding, your baby is basically a tiny soda can ready to fizz over.

Did You Know?
Babies swallow air while feeding, especially from bottles. That's why burping can save you from post-feed meltdowns (and keep your shirt cleaner).

Pro Dad Hack: *Place a burp cloth over your shoulder like you're a fancy waiter, and gently pat the baby's back until you hear that satisfying little 'burp'.*

Key Chapter Takeaways
Though there are various feeding options, breastfeeding is the gold standard. Stay calm during meltdowns: milk explosions, bottle rejections, and late-night chaos are all part of the game. Stay prepared: Set up bottles, formula, and snacks for middle-of-the-night feeds ahead of time. Remember to burb your baby after feeding.

And remember: if you're covered in milk, you're probably doing it right.

CHAPTER 10

Diaper Blowouts & Other Explosive Moments

Welcome to the Diaper Diaries

"Having a baby is like constantly defusing a tiny, stinky bomb."
– Anonymous

If this chapter sounds disgusting, buckle up. It only gets better (or worse, depending on your perspective).

Did You Know?
A healthy newborn averages 10 to 12 diaper changes a day in the first month. That's over 300 diapers a month. Your baby is basically a tiny poop factory!

The Science of Baby Poop

You probably never thought you'd become a poop expert, but here we are. Understanding your baby's poop colors can help you gauge their health.

- **Black:** Sticky, tar-like black poop is normal for a newborn's first stool (meconium). If black stool appears later on, it may signal digested blood from internal bleeding – contact a pediatrician.
- **Brown:** Chocolate-brown poop is a normal, healthy color for babies, especially those on *formula or solid* foods. Various shades of brown indicate that digestion is on track.
- **Yellow:** Mustard-yellow, seedy poop is common and healthy in *breastfed babies*. Bright or watery yellow stool can occur with diarrhea, so monitor for dehydration if it happens.
- **Bright Green:** Bright green (often frothy) poop can occur if a breastfed baby is getting more foremilk than hindmilk (an imbalance) or due to a mild stomach bug. It's usually not serious as long as baby is otherwise well.
- **Dark Green:** Deep green poop is often caused by iron-fortified formula or iron supplements. Babies starting on green veggies may also have dark green stool. This color is usually no cause for concern.
- **Orange:** Poop that's orange in color is typically harmless. It often comes from eating orange-colored foods (like carrots or sweet potatoes) in older babies starting solids.
- **Red:** Reddish poop or red streaks in the stool often mean there's blood present (for example, from a milk allergy, constipation causing an anal fissure, or an intestinal infection). *Red is an abnormal color – have a doctor evaluate any unexplained red stool.*

- **White (Pale Gray):** Pale white or clay-colored poop is *not* normal. It can indicate a lack of bile in the stool (a sign of a liver or gallbladder problem). *If you ever see white or light gray poop, contact the doctor promptly.*
- **Gray:** Ashy or cement-gray poop is another warning sign that something isn't right with digestion (similar to white stool). *Gray stool can occur with bile duct blockages or other issues – it's best to consult a pediatrician.*
- **Blue:** It's very rare to see blue poop in a baby. When it does occur, it's usually due to ingestion of something with strong blue dye (such as food coloring or certain medications). Blue stool by itself isn't typically harmful, *but it's an unusual color – mention it to your doctor if it appears.*

💡 ***Pro Dad Hack:*** *Don't sniff-test diapers directly. Trust your eyes and keep your nose at a safe distance.*

When to Worry

Not all poop is created equal, and as a first-time dad, it's easy to slip into panic mode. Let's clarify.

If the poop is *green, yellow, brown, orange, mustard-seed texture* or if it smells funky but not horrifying, *it's fine.*

Call the pediatrician if you observe:

- black poop (after the first week),
- red streaks (blood),
- white or very pale poop,
- any abnormal color,
- extremely watery, frequent diarrhea,
- baby is refusing to eat or shows signs of dehydration.

Keeping an eye on these colors (as messy as it is!) helps ensure your little one stays healthy.

💡 ***Did You Know?***
Color charts for baby poop exist — and they're shockingly popular! Get one chart for yourself and keep it near the changing table.

The Blowout Phenomenon

Let's address the elephant in the room: *diaper blowouts.*

Blowouts are when poop *escapes* the diaper and ventures out to explore new lands — like your baby's back, your shirt, the car seat, or the dog (yes, it happens).

💡 ***Did You Know?***
According to a 2021 parenting survey, 62% of parents report experiencing a blowout in public within the first 3 months.

💡 ***Pro Dad Hack:*** *Seal the new diaper properly. Loose fasteners = recipe for disaster. Tight but comfy is the magic zone.*

Spotting the Warning Signs

How to predict a blowout? Here's your official early warning system:

- The Face: Scrunched-up eyes, furrowed brow, tomato-red cheeks.
- The Sound: A low rumble, like a motorcycle starting three rooms away.
- The Stillness: Babies weirdly freeze before the storm hits.
- The Smell: You'll know.

Diaper Bag Essentials (The "Go Bag")

Packing a diaper bag is like prepping for a mini-apocalypse. Here's your checklist:

- ☑ Diapers (more than you think you'll need).
- ☑ Wipes (double up).
- ☑ Extra clothes (for baby *and* you).
- ☑ Hand sanitizer.

☑ Plastic bags for dirty diapers (and clothes).

> ***Pro Dad Hack:*** *Restock your diaper bag after every outing. Do not assume it's still loaded.*

Managing Diaper Duties as a Team

Listen, changing diapers isn't glamorous, but sharing the load (pun intended) keeps things fair and prevents meltdowns (yours, not the baby's).

- Take turns.
- Never ever accuse one another. Ever! Doesn't matter how stressed, tired you might be.
- Instead cheer each other on. Remember, you are both playing for the same team (the baby's).
- Make it a game: Who can change faster? Who needs fewer wipes?
- High-five after clean changes. Celebrate small wins.

Sleep-Deprived Mistakes

At some point, you *will* fasten the diaper upside down. Or put it on backward. Or forget the diaper entirely.

"One morning, I was so sleep-deprived," Greg from Arizona confessed, "I changed the baby's diaper, tossed the clean diaper in the trash, and tried to fasten the dirty one back on. My wife laughed for an hour!"

Key Chapter Takeaways

1. Blowouts are inevitable. Stock up on diapers and wipes (seriously, you'll need them).
2. Pack and regularly restock your diaper bag.
3. Print the poop color chart for quick reference.
4. Practice speed changes for emergencies.
5. Team up with your partner to make diaper duty manageable.
6. Keep spare clothes for both you and baby — always.

CHAPTER 11

Baby-Proofing or Panic-Proofing?

How to Keep Your Baby Alive (and Your Sanity Intact)

"Baby-proofing your house is just teaching you how creative your kid can be at finding danger."

– Anonymous

You've entered the wild and wonderful phase of parenting where your baby, once a stationary bundle of cuteness, has transformed into a

roving, giggling wrecking ball with *zero concept of danger* and a *master's degree in chaos.*

One day, you'll blink, and that sweet little bundle will have crawled across the living room, eaten half a magazine, and tried to rewire the television with a fork. Don't panic. (Okay, panic a little).

Baby-proofing isn't just about protecting your kid — it's also about protecting your sanity. And your TV. And your furniture. And your pet hamster.

Let's dive in.

What Actually Needs Baby-Proofing

The Essentials

Let's start with the good news: you do *not* have to bubble-wrap your entire house. Despite what the internet will tell you, you're not preparing for an Olympic crawling competition.

Here's your sanity-saving checklist:

1. **Electrical outlets**: Babies love them, like moths to a flame. Cover them.
2. **Sharp furniture corners**: Your coffee table is basically a medieval weapon. Use corner bumpers.
3. **Stairs**: Install baby gates unless you enjoy spontaneous cardio.
4. **Coins**: Babies want to taste and swallow everything they can get their hands on. Make sure there are no stray coins lying around the house.
5. **Cleaning supplies & meds**: Lock them up tight. Babies don't read warning labels.
6. **Heavy furniture**: Anchor it. Toddlers will try to climb anything like they're auditioning for *American Ninja Warrior: Baby Edition.*

Real-Life Anecdote

Mike from Denver thought he was good until his 8-month-old, Emma, figured out how to open the bottom kitchen drawer and pull out an entire set of measuring cups. "She banged them together like she was leading a parade," Mike said, "I stood there clapping before I realized: wait a minute. Those are metal."

Moral of the story? *If your baby can reach it, they will try to play with it.*

> ***Did You Know?***
> *According to the CDC, household injuries are the leading cause of death in children under 3 years old, but most are preventable with basic safety measures. No need for a full panic attack — just some smart choices.*

Safety Myths vs. Real Risks

Myth #1: If I baby-proof everything, my baby can't get hurt.
LOL! Babies are like tiny Houdinis. If there's a way, they'll find it. Baby-proofing *reduces* risk, but no setup is foolproof.

Myth #2: Walkers help babies learn to walk.
Nope! Walkers are basically rolling hazard zones. In fact, Canada has banned them because of injury risks. Floor play is safer and better for motor development.

Myth #3: Expensive gear = safer baby.
Not always. Safety is about design and proper use, not price tags. A cheap outlet cover protects just as well as a fancy one.

Real-Life Anecdote

Chris from Austin spent $300 on a baby monitor with 'temperature control, humidity tracker, lullaby options, and facial recognition'. His baby, Noah, still rolled under the crib and fell asleep there. The monitor kept alerting Chris that the temperature was optimal!

Moral of the story? *Tech is great, but eyes-on parenting wins.*

Easy Ways to Create a Safe Environment

Step 1: Get low

Yup. Time to crawl around your house like you're reenacting an army boot camp scene. From this low vantage point, you'll see what your baby sees:

- Exposed cords?
- Loose change?
- Dog food bowl looking like a snack buffet?

Fix them before your baby finds them!

Step 2: Think like a baby

Babies are curious. Imagine you're seeing the world for the first time. Shiny things? Irresistible. Dangly cords? Must pull. Pets? Must hug (violently).

Keep temptation out of reach.

Step 3: Create safe zones

Rather than obsessively baby-proofing the whole house, create safe zones.

Example: Playpen in the living room. Baby gate in the kitchen doorway. Now you can cook dinner without your little explorer pulling pots onto its head.

> ***Did You Know?***
> *Data shows that creating 'safe zones' reduces household accidents by nearly 40% in the first year of mobility. (Source: National Safety Council.)*

Try This Now!

Crawl around your house. Yes, really, do it now! You'll feel silly at first, but soon you'll spot all kinds of hidden dangers from your baby's point of view.

Dad's Common Safety Slip-Ups (And How to Avoid Them)

1. **The 'I'll do it later' trap**
   Procrastination is the enemy. Babies grow faster than your to-do list. If you notice a hazard, fix it *now*, not 'this weekend'.

2. **Overlooking bathroom dangers**
   Water + baby = danger zone. Always keep the bathroom door locked, toilet lids closed and install latches on cabinets with cleaning supplies.
3. **Forgetting visitor awareness**
   Grandparents love to visit but often forget their reading glasses on low tables. Small objects like hearing aids or pill bottles? Baby magnets.

Real-Life Anecdote

Greg from Chicago hosted a family barbecue. "My mother-in-law left her purse open, and our son Tyler found a packet of sugar-free gum," Greg says. "FYI, xylitol is toxic to babies. Luckily, we caught him mid-chew!"

Lesson? *Make 'visitor sweep' part of your routine.*

Baby-Proofing Self-Assessment

Rate (from 1-10) how confident you feel about each area of your home. Don't overthink — just trust your gut!

Area	Confidence (1 = Disaster Waiting to Happen, 10 = Fort Knox)
Living Room Safety	☐ 1 ☐ 2 ☐ 3 ☐ 4 ☐ 5 ☐ 6 ☐ 7 ☐ 8 ☐ 9 ☐ 10
Kitchen Hazards	☐ 1 ☐ 2 ☐ 3 ☐ 4 ☐ 5 ☐ 6 ☐ 7 ☐ 8 ☐ 9 ☐ 10
Electrical Outlets	☐ 1 ☐ 2 ☐ 3 ☐ 4 ☐ 5 ☐ 6 ☐ 7 ☐ 8 ☐ 9 ☐ 10
Furniture Stability	☐ 1 ☐ 2 ☐ 3 ☐ 4 ☐ 5 ☐ 6 ☐ 7 ☐ 8 ☐ 9 ☐ 10
Visitor Hazard Awareness	☐ 1 ☐ 2 ☐ 3 ☐ 4 ☐ 5 ☐ 6 ☐ 7 ☐ 8 ☐ 9 ☐ 10
Bathroom Safety	☐ 1 ☐ 2 ☐ 3 ☐ 4 ☐ 5 ☐ 6 ☐ 7 ☐ 8 ☐ 9 ☐ 10

Scoring Tip:

- 40–60 points: You're a Safety Superstar!
- 25–39 points: Not bad, but do another sweep.
- Below 25: Let's start crawling around your house. Again.

Key Chapter Takeaways

Every time you spot a hazard and fix it, you're keeping your little human safe *and* becoming a better dad. Not a perfect dad — a real one. Remember:

- Not everything needs baby-proofing. Prioritize the real dangers.
- Expensive gear isn't always safer.
- Think like a baby: crawl around and see the world from their view.
- Create safe zones to manage chaos.
- Visitor hazards are real — do a sweep.

CHAPTER 12

The Screaming Potato: Why Babies Cry for No Reason

Decoding the Mystery of Endless Crying Without Losing Your Mind

> *"Babies cry for three reasons: hunger, discomfort, and just to mess with you."*
>
> — Anonymous

If you've ever had the panicked thought, "Why is my baby crying like the world is ending?" — well, the bad news is, this will not be the last time.

Here's something no one tells you: *crying is your baby's main form of communication.* Imagine waking up in a strange place with no language, no mobility, and every bodily function out of your control. You'd probably cry too!

> ***Did You Know?***
> *All babies cry. In fact, it's typical for a newborn to cry 1 to 4 hours a day.*
> *– Mayoclinic.org*

Real-Life Anecdote

Martin recollects the first time his daughter, Emma, unleashed her lungs at 3:47 a.m. "I honestly thought we had accidentally brought home a car alarm with a human face. She went from peaceful, angelic sleep to full-blown, apocalyptic wailing in two seconds flat. I stared at her, she stared at me (while still screaming), and I had this terrifying realization: I have no idea what I'm doing."

Why Babies Cry?

Let's look at some root causes.

1. **Hunger**

   The most common reason. Imagine going six hours without food and not knowing words yet.

   > ***Pro Dad Hack:*** *If the baby is crying its lungs out for more than an hour or so, try feeding it first. Also, sucking comforts babies, so keep a pacifier handy.*

2. **Discomfort**

   Wet diaper? Tags poking? Swaddle too tight? Babies are basically the CEOs of Sensory Overreaction, LLC.

3. **Gas**

   Yep. Babies are like old cars — lots of backfiring. Except cuter.

4. **Lack of sleep**
   A baby who doesn't get its daily quota of sleep will not be a very happy baby and makes sure that you know.

   Did You Know?
   As per a study by the National Sleep Foundation, newborns need 14–17 hours of sleep a day — but they rarely get it in one peaceful stretch.

5. **Over-stimulation**
   Do you know how you feel at loud weddings with strobe lights? That's your baby in a crowded grocery store.

6. **Under-stimulation**
   On the flip side, babies also cry when they're bored. Yep, your tiny boss needs just the right amount of action.

7. **Just because…**
   Honestly, sometimes there's no good reason. Babies have rough days too. Maybe they're teething, maybe they're working through existential diaper issues. And they are not exactly overflowing with patience.
   Babies know the power of their screams on you and *because they can.*

Real-Life Anecdote
Mark, a first-time dad from Ohio, told me he once spent a solid hour flying a spoon like an airplane into his daughter's mouth, only for her to scream harder with every 'zoom'. Desperate, he abandoned the spoon, picked up an actual toy airplane, and pretended to 'land it' into the mashed peas. She stopped crying instantly, smiled, and ate the whole bowl.

Moral of the story? *Babies are weird!*

Is It an Emergency… or Just Drama?

The hardest part? Figuring out if it's a real emergency or your baby is just doing an Oscar-worthy performance.

Here's a simple rule of thumb:

- **Sharp, sudden, high-pitched wails?** Check for immediate issues (pain, illness).
- **Rhythmic, escalating cries?** Probably hunger or sleepiness.
- **Whiny, fussy sounds?** Your baby is bored or overstimulated.

Always trust your gut. If you're ever in doubt, call your pediatrician.

Real-Life Anecdote

Tyler from Kansas swore he'd memorized every reason his newborn son cried. One night, the baby erupted into screams that didn't fit any pattern. Tyler and his wife checked everything. Clean diaper? Check. Bottle? Check. Gas relief? Check. Finally, they discovered the culprit: the pacifier had fallen *next to* the crib, and their son could *see* it but couldn't reach it.

💡 Pro Dad Hacks for Crying Calamities

Let's arm you with a few battlefield-tested tricks:

1. The 5 S's by Dr. Harvey Karp:

i. Swaddle
Wrap your baby in a soft blanket for warmth and comfort. It helps them feel secure—like how they were curled up inside the womb. Bonus: It also prevents flailing arms from waking them up.

ii. Side or Stomach Position
Hold your baby on their side or stomach (but always remember to put them on their back to sleep to avoid risk of suffocation!). This position often helps them feel more settled and eases gas or discomfort.

iii. Shush
Make a strong "shhh" sound near their ear—louder than you think! It mimics the whooshing noise of blood flow in the womb and has a magical calming effect.

iv. Swing
Gently rock, bounce, or sway your baby. Think small, quick movements like in the womb—not big carnival ride motions. Baby carriers, arms, or swings can help.

v. Suck
   Let your baby suck on something—a pacifier, a clean finger, or during feeding. Sucking is super soothing and helps calm their nervous system.

2. White Noise Apps
Play sounds like rainfall, ocean waves, or vacuum cleaners.

3. The Magic Bounce
Hold the baby securely and gently bounce on your heels. Don't question it. It works.

4. Go for a Drive
There's something about the hum of the car engine. Warning: you might fall asleep too (so make sure you've got backup).

5. The Shower Trick
No, not for you. Turn on the bathroom fan and shower to create soothing white noise.

Real-Life Anecdote
Chris, a dad from Chicago, accidentally discovered the magic of white noise when he was vacuuming while his daughter was wailing. She stopped mid-cry and stared at the vacuum like it was the Mona Lisa. Desperate, Chris vacuumed the same spot on the living room carpet for 25 straight minutes until she fell asleep.

His carpet is now spotless.

When to Worry Without Panicking

While most crying is normal, there *are* times when you should call your pediatrician:

1. Fever (over 100.4°F for babies under 3 months).
2. Signs of illness (vomiting, diarrhea, rash).
3. If your baby's cry sounds strange or weak.
4. If they're inconsolable for hours (yes, even for babies).

When in doubt, just call. Pediatricians are pros at decoding worried first-time dad calls. Remember, there's no such thing as a dumb question when it comes to your kid.

Closing Thoughts

Crying feels endless, but here's some good news: it gets better. No, really. One day, you'll notice the cries taper off, and your little one will start communicating in ways that don't involve high-decibel shrieking.

CHAPTER 13

Public Enemy #1: Tiny and Loud

Because Nothing Tests Your Patience (and Public Speaking Skills) Like a Screaming Child in the Middle of Aisle Seven

> *"You don't know embarrassment until you've tried to calm a screaming baby with 87 strangers staring at you."*
>
> — Anonymous Dad, somewhere in Target

You're finally brave enough to take your baby out in public. You even remembered the diaper bag. Things are going smoothly. For a brief, shining moment, you feel like you've got this whole parenting thing under control.

And then… it begins.

The fussing.

The face scrunch.

The red cheeks.

The ear-piercing shriek that echoes off the linoleum like a fire alarm in a high school hallway.

Congratulations! You've unlocked your *baby's first public meltdown!*

In this chapter, we'll explore why this happens, how to survive it with your sanity intact, and how to earn your unofficial "Dad of the Year" badge in the middle of Aisle Seven — or at 30,000 feet above sea level.

Why Babies Lose It in Public Places

Why do babies choose the most public, inconvenient moments to turn into tiny banshees? *Sensory Overload.*

Babies are like brand-new iPhones with too many apps running at once. Bright lights, loud noises, strangers' faces, and the overwhelming smell of the deli counter can fry their circuits.

> 💡 ***Did You Know?***
> *Babies process new sensory information at double the rate of adults, which is why they can get overwhelmed much faster. (Source: American Academy of Pediatrics)*

Timing is Everything (And It's Always the Worst)

Public meltdowns usually strike when:

- They're hungry.
- They're tired.
- They've just filled their diaper like a frosting bag.

Combine any two of these, and you've got a recipe for disaster.

Babies are tiny drama kings and queens. They express every feeling at full volume. There is no filter, there is only *maximum amplification.*

Your Dad Survival Toolkit

1. Snacks (For Both of You)

If your baby is old enough, pack easy snacks. Puffs, teething biscuits, or a quick bottle can buy you precious quiet time.

Also, grab a protein bar for yourself. Parenting on an empty stomach turns *you* into the cranky one.

2. Distractions Galore

- Crinkly toys
- Teething rings
- A small book
- Literally anything safe within grabbing distance

Babies are easily confused characters, so rotate distractions like a magician pulling endless scarves out of a hat.

3. Quick Comfort Items

Keep a light blanket or soft lovey handy. Babies love familiar textures and smells when they're in unfamiliar places.

4. Calm Balm

Your own calm energy is a secret weapon. Babies are like little emotional mirrors — if you panic, they panic more. Breathe deep, stay loose, and keep your tone gentle, even if you're dying inside.

Dealing with 'The Audience': The Three Nightmare Scenarios

Let's tackle the three nightmare scenarios, step by step.

Scenario 1: Screaming Baby at 30,000 Feet (The Flying Meltdown)

There you are, trapped in a metal tube with 200 strangers, and your baby decides it's time for a sonic boom. Preparation is power.

Pack smart:

- Extra diapers and wipes (double what you think you'll need).
- Bottles or snacks ready for takeoff and landing (sucking eases ear pressure).
- Toys that don't make annoying sounds (unless you *want* to make enemies).

Mid-Air Meltdown Protocol

1. Stay calm. Babies feel your stress. If you tense up, so will they.
2. Walk the Aisle. Gentle motion helps, and so does removing your baby from their cramped seat.
3. Enlist allies. Flight attendants are miracle workers — they've seen it all. Smile, and they'll likely offer help (or at least extra napkins for your sweat).

> ***Did You Know?***
> *Babies' ears are super sensitive to cabin pressure changes, especially during takeoff and landing, which can lead to crying. Feeding during ascent and descent can help regulate that pressure. (Source: FAA Child Safety Recommendations)*

Real-Life Anecdote

Meet Mike. Mike took his 7-month-old on a cross-country flight. Baby Emma began screaming somewhere over Kansas. Mike, a rookie dad, panicked at first. But then, a flight attendant handed him a cup with ice.

Turns out, shaking ice in a plastic cup is baby hypnotism. Emma calmed immediately.

Scenario 2: Screaming Baby in the Grocery Aisle

The grocery store meltdown is a special kind of horror. You just needed milk and diapers. Suddenly, you're standing frozen in Aisle Seven while your baby sounds like a malfunctioning car alarm.

Step 1: Assess the Situation Fast

- Hungry? Thirsty? Wet diaper?
- Sensory overload from bright lights or jingles?

Step 2: Activate Distract Mode

- Hand baby your grocery list or (clean) car keys.
- Narrate your shopping trip: "Ooooh, look at these green apples!"
- If all else fails, grab an emergency snack — many stores let you feed your child while you shop.

Step 3: Ignore the blackmail (and the stares)

If all else fails, then the baby is probably howling to blackmail you and get something in return. Because they know intuitively that you can't bear to see them howl. And when the baby sees that you don't care about the blackmail, it realises that its game is up and will give up eventually.

> *"Courage is not the absence of panic. It's carrying on with your head high while holding a screaming baby and three bags of groceries."*
>
> — Every Parent, Everywhere

Real-Life Anecdote

David, a dad of two, was once cornered in the cereal aisle when his toddler began wailing at the injustice of not getting marshmallow cereal. Jenna calmly scooped his child up, walked to the quietest corner of the store (near the canned peas), and softly sang 'Wheels on the Bus.' After three verses and some bouncing, the storm passed.

Scenario 3: Baby Meltdown During "Impress the Important Guest" Moment

Imagine this: your boss is over for dinner. Or maybe it's your in-laws who already suspect your parenting skills. You're pouring water, making polite conversation, trying your best to make a decent impression.

And your baby chooses this exact moment to let loose a scream so loud, it rattles the cutlery.

Here's what you can do to salvage the situation.

1. Accept the inevitable

Understand this is going to happen at least once in your dad career. Timing is never in your favour. Children are predictably unpredictable (read: chaotic). And guests, even judgmental ones, know this deep down.

2. The Swift intervention

Smile (no matter how awkward). Pick up your baby and gently remove them from the scene, even if just to another room. Whisper reassurances and try light rocking.

3. Use humor

"Well, someone's not impressed with my lasagna!" A bit of humor goes a long way in disarming the tension!

4. Play the long game

If the meltdown persists, excuse yourself gracefully. Prioritize your baby's comfort over appearances — people will respect that, even if they don't say so.

> ***Did You Know?***
> *Studies show that adults are generally more forgiving of babies crying than parents expect — it's the parents' perception of others' judgment that heightens the stress. (Source: Journal of Child Development, 2020)*

Try This Now!
Think back to a time you felt flustered in public (maybe a speech or sports game). What helped you manage your nerves? Apply the same tactics next time you face a public meltdown.

Closing Thoughts
Here's the truth: no one expects you to have a magic solution to every baby meltdown. But showing up, staying calm, and doing your best? That's winning.

So go ahead. Face the meltdown head-on. Smile at the scowling stranger. Whisper to your baby, *"Bring it on, kiddo!"*

Key Chapter Takeaways
Accept that public meltdowns will happen (consider yourself very lucky if it doesn't). Here's a quick summary:

1. Preparation is your best friend.
2. Stay calm.
3. Use distraction techniques.
4. If all else fails, ignore the baby's blackmail.
5. Use humor.

Collect stories that you'll laugh about later (much later). And next time you see another parent in the same boat, give them the secret "I've been there" nod.

CHAPTER 14

The Third Wheel: Mom, Baby… and You

Becoming More Than Just the Guy Who Assembles the Crib

"A father is someone who carries pictures where his money used to be."
– Unknown

Did You Know?
According to a 2022 survey by Fatherly, over 58% of new dads reported feeling 'marginalized' or 'out of the loop' in the first few months of parenting.

That's more than half of us wandering around, wondering if we're supposed to be doing something other than making another pot of coffee.

The thing is, newborns are biologically wired to gravitate toward their primary caregiver (usually mom). It's nothing personal — they're just playing the odds for survival. In those early weeks, it might feel like you're an understudy in the play of your own life.

Pro Dad Hack: Reframe Your Role
Instead of seeing yourself as an assistant, start thinking of yourself as a co-pilot. Sure, your partner might be Captain Milkybar, but you're handling navigation, turbulence control, and emotional safety briefings.
Use this mantra: "I'm not just helping — I'm parenting." Repeat as often as needed.

How to Actually Bond with Your Baby (Even When You Feel Like a Stranger)

Babies aren't the most encouraging companions at first. They stare, they cry, and they poop like tiny printers running out of toner. But *bonding is a process — not an event.*

And guess what? You have more tools than you think.

Tool 1: Your voice.
Babies recognize your voice from the womb. In fact, research from the University of Washington shows newborns can recognize their father's voice within days of birth. So, talk to them. Narrate your day. Sing your favorite (clean) rap lyrics.

Tool 2: Skin-to-skin contact.
Don't let moms have all the fun. Strip down to your chest and hold your baby against you. Skin-to-skin boosts bonding hormones like oxytocin — for both of you.

Tool 3: Playtime is Dad time.
Once your baby hits about 2-3 months, playtime is prime dad territory. Rough-and-tumble play (gentle, of course) helps babies develop motor skills and trust.

> ***Did You Know?***
> *Studies show that babies whose dads engage in playful activities tend to develop better problem-solving skills and higher self-esteem. (Source: Journal of Child Development, 2021)*

Real-Life Anecdote
Tom, a new dad from Texas, couldn't carry a tune to save his life. Still, in the dead of night, he'd hum Bruce Springsteen songs while rocking his daughter. To his surprise, she'd stop crying. His theory? "She was either soothed by the music or confused into silence."

The Ultimate Dad-Baby Bonding Ideas That Actually Work

1. **The Classic Walk-and-Talk:** Strap on a baby carrier and take a stroll. Narrate the neighborhood like you're hosting a travel show.
2. **The Expressive Face Game:** Babies love exaggerated expressions. Raise your eyebrows, stick out your tongue, and watch your baby try to copy you.
3. **The Dance Party:** Crank up some music and dance around with your baby. Silly moves encouraged. Bonus points if you wear sunglasses indoors.
4. **The Bath Time Buddy:** Team up for bath time. It's a splashy bonding session (just keep towels handy).

5. **The Read-Aloud Routine:** Reading to your baby, even if it's the back of a cereal box, builds connection and language skills. Plus, you get to practice your dramatic voice.

When Your Partner Takes the Lead (And You're Wondering What to Do)

It's natural to feel sidelined, especially if your partner is doing a lot of the heavy lifting (like, you know, feeding the baby with her actual body). But this is your chance to shine in supporting roles that matter.

> 💡 ***Pro Dad Hack:*** *Communication is king. Ask, "What's something I can take off your plate today?" This line works like magic.*
>
> *And if you notice tensions rising, remember: Sleep deprivation turns saints into sarcastic goblins.*

Helping Without Hovering

Here's where things get a little tricky. You want to help your partner, but you also don't want to become the shadow lurking behind her every move, asking, "Are you sure you're holding the bottle at the right angle?"

Nobody likes the backseat driver of parenting. Instead,

- Be available, not intrusive.
- Listen before leaping into action.
- Offer to take a shift — and mean it.

> 💡 ***Pro Dad Hack: The 'Invisible Hero' Approach***
>
> *Do the things that need doing without making a big announcement. Wipe the counter, change the diaper, soothe the baby at 3 a.m. without waiting for applause. You'll quietly become the MVP of the house.*

Try This Now!

Time yourself narrating a five-minute play-by-play of your current activity to your baby and watch your baby's expressions closely.

Done? Give yourself a pat on your back. Now try out this weekly action plan below.

Day 1: Narrate your day to the baby.
Day 2: Try the expressive face game.
Day 3: Plan a solo stroller walk.
Day 4: Help with bath time.
Day 5: Sing a silly song at bedtime.
Day 6: Reflect on the week's funniest parenting moments.
Day 7: Celebrate your progress.

Closing Thoughts

Feeling like the third wheel is normal, but you're a crucial part of this parenting team. Bonding with your baby happens in small, silly, meaningful moments. Support your partner without hovering — be the silent MVP.

CHAPTER 15

From Hot Dates to Hot Messes

Keeping the Love Alive When Romance Feels Like a Myth

"Date night now involves diapers, burp cloths, and falling asleep at 9 p.m."

– Every New Parent

Remember the spontaneous date nights? Midnight ice cream runs? Lazy Sunday mornings?

Yeah… those have now been replaced by milk-stained shirts, bleary-eyed 'conversations', and debates about who's more sleep-deprived.

But fear not. This chapter is your survival manual to keep the romance alive when life feels like one long episode of *Survivor: Diaper Island.*

> ***Did You Know?***
> *A study by the Gottman Institute found that 67% of couples reported a decrease in their relationship satisfaction during the first three years of parenthood. (Source: Gottman Institute, 2015)*

Real-Life Anecdote

"Sleep deprivation does dangerous things to your brain. I thought I'd spice things up with a flirty text to my wife while she was out getting groceries. Something like "Can't wait to get you alone later!" to keep the spark alive.

Except, in my zombie state, I accidentally sent it to the family group chat. Grandma replied first: 'Excited for you too! Remember to hydrate.' My brother sent a meme of a fire extinguisher. My father-in-law? Radio silence (to this day).

— Kevin, Dad of Two

Quick Romance Hacks

Forget grand gestures. Right now, romance is about tiny wins. *Micro-moments.*

1. Coffee love notes

If you're up first (you probably are), scribble a sweet note and leave it by the coffee machine. Extra points if you actually make the coffee.

2. Text flirting

Send a flirty (but safe-for-work) message during the day.

Example: "Can't wait to see you tonight. Maybe we can fold laundry... together."

3. Steal a 5-minute dance
Put on your wedding song, grab your partner, and sway in the kitchen for five minutes.

4. Compliment without baby talk
Instead of, "You're such a great mom," say, "You're amazing. And you look incredible today."

Remember, they're a person, not just the co-parent.

Try This Now!
Compliment your partner without mentioning the baby.

Examples:

- *"Your laugh still gives me butterflies."*
- *"You crushed it today."*
- *"Have I told you today how much I love you?"*

Notice how your partner lights up.

Real-Life Anecdote
"We hadn't been out of the house together in weeks. Not even to the mailbox. Cabin fever was real. So, one night after the baby finally fell asleep, I looked at my wife and said, 'Let's go on a date… to the car.'

We grabbed the baby monitor, our favorite snacks, and sat in the car parked in the driveway. No destination. No screaming baby. Just two exhausted parents, blasting our favorite music from before the baby arrived.

We sat there for 45 glorious minutes, eating chocolate, laughing about absolutely nothing, and pretending we were teenagers again. It wasn't fancy, but it was free, it didn't require babysitting, and nobody cried (except maybe from laughing too hard).

It's now our weird little tradition whenever things get too crazy."

— Alex, Dad of Twins

Communication Tips (For When You're Too Tired to Talk)

Exhaustion makes communication feel like decoding ancient hieroglyphics. You're both operating on 3% battery life. But this is when communication matters most.

1. Do *not* accuse

Avoid sweeping accusatory words like, "You always...!" or "You never...!" Instead, try: "I feel exhausted. Can we figure this out together?"

2. Use the magic question

Ask: "What can I do to make today a little easier for you?"
Simple. Effective. Brownie points galore.

3. Bed check-in rituals

Every night, even if it's just 2 minutes before collapsing, ask:

"How are you holding up?"

"What was the best part of your day?"

This reminds you both that you're a team, not just two overworked zookeepers for your tiny human.

Real- Life Anecdote

"One night, I thought I'd be a hero. My wife had been running on two hours of sleep for three days straight, and I wanted to do something nice. I set up this 'spa night' at home: dim lights, calming music, fancy bath salts I found in the back of the cupboard.

I got the baby to sleep (miracle!), drew her a bath, and even found her favorite candle — although I didn't realize it had been buried under the changing table. When I lit it, it smelled suspiciously like baby wipes.

Just as she stepped into the tub, the baby monitor let out this ungodly screech. Baby was up, game over!

We ended up both dunking our feet in the bath while holding the baby between us, taking turns rocking her to sleep. Not exactly the spa night I planned, but honestly? Still a win. Sort of. Okay, half a win."

— Jared, first time dad

Did You Know?

- *Couples who laugh together are more likely to stay together. Laughter triggers feel-good hormones like oxytocin—the same hormone that bonds parents and babies! (Source: Mayo Clinic)*
- *Mini gestures matter. According to relationship expert Dr. John Gottman, successful couples have a ratio of 5 positive interactions for every 1 negative one.*

Try This Now!

Take 5 minutes to jot these down with your partner

Question	***Your Answer***
What's one small thing that makes you feel loved?	
How can we steal 10 minutes for us this week?	
What's a fun pre-baby thing we can recreate at home?	
How can we appreciate each other daily, even if exhausted?	

Bonus: Stick this on your fridge. Refer to it in moments of chaos.

When All Else Fails, Laugh

If you can't fix it, laugh at it. Humour is a secret weapon in the trenches of new parenthood.

Golden Rule: Laugh at yourself and NOT at your partner unless you are willing to risk a visit to the local hospital.

Real-Life Anecdote

"Our first attempt at 'date night' post-baby was watching a movie on the couch. We both woke up to the end credits. Best nap ever!"

— James, Dad of Two

Closing Thoughts

Sure, date nights now involve burp cloths and yawns, but they're still date nights. Keep showing up, keep laughing. This wild, messy, exhausting chapter is just the beginning of a love story with some epic plot twists. Remember:

1. Your relationship will change—and that's okay.
2. Tiny romantic gestures beat grand ones in the newborn phase.
3. Communicate like you're on the same team (because you are).
4. Laugh together. Humour saves relationships.
5. Steal moments for connecting with each other, whenever you can. Even 2 minutes count.

~

CHAPTER 16

Where Did My Life Go?

How to Still Have Hobbies, Friends, and a Tiny Bit of Sanity

"Your hobbies now include diaper changing, sleep deprivation, and becoming a human pacifier."

– Every Dad Ever

You used to have hobbies. Friends. Maybe even abs.

Now you have baby wipes in your wallet and an exciting new social life at aisle seven of Target.

This chapter is your roadmap to dig out your old life and feel like yourself again—at least a little bit.

Did You Know?

According to a 2022 survey by the Pew Research Center, new dads report a 60% drop in personal leisure time during the first year of parenthood!

Getting back your life (or at least trying to)

Step 1: Acceptance

Pre-baby, free time looked like this: "I think I'll go play golf this afternoon."

Post-baby, free time looks like: "The baby is asleep. I have 12 minutes. Do I shower or eat a cookie?"

Both are valid choices. Both will feel like *luxury vacations.*

The first step is accepting that hobbies and friendships now fit into odd-shaped gaps in your day, like playing Tetris with your schedule.

Real-Life Anecdote

Take my buddy Greg, for example. Greg loved mowing his lawn—it was his peaceful ritual. After his son was born, mowing became his excuse to escape.

One day, his wife caught him 'mowing' the already-cut grass... *for the third time that week.*

Step 2: Micro-hobbies are your new best friends

Gone are the days of eight-hour fishing trips or entire weekends lost to fantasy football drafts.

Now it's about *bite-sized* hobbies that fit between naps (the baby's and yours).

Here are some low hanging fruits:

- Read one chapter of a book, not the whole thing.
- Do a 10-minute workout.
- Groove to a 3-minute music video.

> **Pro Dad Hack:** *Leave hobby materials everywhere. Guitar in the living room. Dumbbells next to the crib. Sketchpad in the bathroom. Remember, environment is more powerful than will power.*

Real-Life Anecdote

My cousin Mike, an ex-model airplane hobbyist, tried to pick up his old passion after his daughter arrived. Six months in, the poor guy had built half a wing and painted exactly three windows before his baby discovered the joy of chewing on tiny plastic propellers.

Now, he calls it his '18-year project'. He jokes, "I'll finish it when she leaves for college... if my eyesight holds up."

Step 3: Text that friend

You know that friend you haven't talked to in weeks because your life is a never-ending loop of feeding, burping, and diapering?

Text him. Better yet, text five of them. Friendships don't die after you have a kid—they just hibernate like bears in winter. You need these guys more than ever.

Try This Now!

Text an old friend. See if they still recognize you.

Step 4: Embrace the power of 'me time'

Let's get one thing straight: *You are allowed to take time for yourself.*

This is not selfish. It's self-preservation. Think of it like airplane safety instructions: put your oxygen mask on first before helping others.

The better you care for yourself, the better dad you'll be. Even if that means disappearing for 20 minutes to eat a sandwich in your car while listening to sports radio.

Step 5: Lower the bar
Before your baby, you may have had goals like:
- Run a marathon.
- Learn French.
- Brew your own beer.

Post-baby, your goals are more like:
- Shower every other day.
- Reheat coffee less than three times.
- Don't wear your shirt inside out at work.

Celebrate these wins! Progress is progress.

Step 6: Seek help
Call in reinforcements from family or friends. It's not weakness—it's wisdom. Trade time like precious currency. Because it is. Even 30 minutes every Sunday morning is good.

Step 7: Remember, this is temporary
Right now, life feels like one endless baby loop. But babies grow up faster than you think.

One day you'll blink, and the baby who screamed through the night will be begging you to watch them play soccer or teach them to ride a bike.

You'll have time for your hobbies again. You'll go out with friends and not worry about leaking bottles or diaper bags. Until then, celebrate the tiny wins and hang in there.

> ***Did You Know?***
> *Studies show that hobbies reduce stress hormones by up to 68%.*

Real-Life Anecdote
Chris, took up birdwatching after his twins were born. Not because he loved birds.

In his words, "I sit outside with binoculars and pretend I'm deeply invested in the migration patterns of sparrows. In reality, I'm just enjoying *the silence!*"

Key Chapter Takeaways

Here's a quick recap:

- Your hobbies still matter. Even if they're bite-sized now.
- Friends are your lifeline. Text them, call them.
- 'Me time' isn't optional—it's essential.
- Lower the bar and celebrate tiny victories.
- This phase won't last forever.

CHAPTER 17

Keeping Up with the Dad-Joneses

Why Your Parenting Style Will Never Be Good Enough for the Internet

"The only thing more competitive than a toddler at a playground? Other parents online."

– Anonymous

After becoming a dad, your social media feed is going crazy. It feels like every other parent out there is either raising a baby Einstein or running a small, Instagram-worthy farm in their backyard.

Meanwhile, you're just trying to remember if you brushed your teeth today.

In this chapter, we will learn how to dodge the comparison trap, and help you embrace your gloriously imperfect, real-life version of fatherhood.

Real-Life Anecdote

Jason, a first-time dad from Ohio, saw an ad online for a 'Dad Bod to Rad Bod' challenge. He signed up immediately. They promised six-pack abs in six weeks, even with a newborn at home.

Week one, Jason managed to do three push-ups (while his baby was strapped to him in a carrier, crying). Week two, his baby projectile spit up all over his workout mat. Week three? He traded the gym for extra sleep. In Jason's words, "No six-pack is worth dying from exhaustion."

Lesson? *Dad bod is not a flaw, it's a survival badge.*

All that glitters is not gold

No one posts about the diaper blowouts at 3 a.m. No one shares their toddler's full-body meltdown in the cereal aisle. No one live-streams the moment they realize they're out of wipes mid-diaper change.

What you see online are the *greatest hits*, with all the bloopers conveniently edited out.

> ***Did You Know?***
> *A 2022 study by the American Psychological Association found that a whopping 62% of new parents reported feeling "inadequate" after viewing parenting content on social media!*

The Danger of Comparison (Spoiler Alert: It's Useless)

Here's the thing about parenting: *you're only competing with yourself.*

Not with 'Fitness Dad' on Instagram who claims he lost his dad bod in six weeks.

You are raising your kid, in your house, with your life circumstances. Your parenting style is unique because your context is unique. Some dads are hands-on swaddlers, others become diaper ninjas. Some are baby-wearing champions at Target, and some are stroller stunt drivers in the park.

There is no 'right' way.

> *"Don't compare your behind-the-scenes to someone else's highlight reel."*
>
> – Steven Furtick

Real-Life Anecdote

Greg, from Texas, couldn't get his newborn to sleep no matter what he tried. Lullabies? Fail. White noise? Fail.

Out of desperation, Greg started reading aloud whatever was nearby — cereal boxes, tax documents, even the instruction manual for his lawnmower. Surprisingly, it worked! His baby was out like a light every time he hit paragraph 2 of 'Proper Spark Plug Maintenance'.

> Lesson? *If it works for your baby, it works. Period. Even if it looks ridiculous.*

The Power of the Dad Squad

Here's something wildly underrated: *dad friends.*

You need a squad — a brotherhood of equally sleep-deprived, confused, caffeine-fuelled dads who understand exactly what you're going through.

Dad squads are not about perfection. They're about survival, sanity, and swapping hilarious horror stories.

Real-Life Anecdote

Ryan, a new dad from Chicago, accidentally started a 'diaper hotline' with three of his dad friends. Every time one of them faced a particularly catastrophic diaper blowout, they sent a warning text to the group: "Code Brown. Full coverage. Send prayers."

What started as a joke turned into daily check-ins, meme exchanges, and even late-night pep talks.

Today, they've expanded the hotline to include feeding fails, sleep regressions, and spontaneous dad jokes.

Ryan says, "It's the best accidental support group I never knew I needed".

Try This Now!

Rate yourself (1–10) on the Dad's Parenting Confidence Scorecard below

Statement	***Score (1-10)***
I can ignore perfect parents on social media without flinching.	
I remind myself daily that I'm doing my best, even if it looks messy.	
I laugh at parenting fails (especially my own).	
I've talked to another dad about my parenting doubts.	
I celebrate small victories (like catching spit-up with a burp cloth).	

Your Total Score: *______ / 50*

Results:

- ***40–50:*** *Dad Jedi – You've mastered the art of not giving a hoot about online parenting perfection.*
- ***25–39:*** *Dad Warrior – You're doing great, just dodge a few more social media traps.*
- ***Below 25:*** *Dad in Progress – Don't worry, we all start here. Keep laughing and leaning on your squad.*

Closing Thoughts

No one has this parenting thing perfectly figured out including your high school buddy who only posts sunset family pics. Social media is not real life, comparison is a waste of your precious sleep-deprived energy. Your baby doesn't care if you haven't mastered the art of organic food puree or coordinated family outfits. Your kid only cares that you show up, messy and exhausted but full of love.

And frankly, that's worth a thousand social media likes.

~

CHAPTER 18

Am I Screwing This Kid Up?

Feeling Bad About Feeling Bad About Feeling Bad

"There is no such thing as a perfect parent, so just be a real one."

— Sue Atkins

If you're reading this chapter, you've already felt it. That tiny voice in your head whispering "You should've done more!" Or "Why did you say that in front of the baby? He's already scarred for life!"

Welcome to the Dad Guilt Spiral.

Dad guilt is like the playlist you didn't ask for but keeps *looping* anyway with the same three tracks:

1. *"Am I doing enough?"*
2. *"Am I doing it right?"*
3. *"Did I just permanently mess up my baby?"*

Did You Know?
A 2022 study from the Journal of Family Psychology found that 83% of first-time dads experience 'performance anxiety' about parenting.

The Universal Dad Fear: Am I Messing This Up?

Why this fear and guilt?

- **Inexperience:** You've never done this before.
- **Overload of (conflicting) advice:** Aunt Susan swears by one method. Instagram suggests another. YouTube offers seventeen alternatives.
- **Responsibility overload:** You're not just responsible for keeping the baby alive. You're responsible for raising a *decent human being.* No pressure.

Real-Life Anecdote

Jason, a new dad in Texas, decided to take charge of bath time while his wife got some rest. Five minutes in, he texted her in all caps:

"THE BABY SLIPPED LIKE A BAR OF SOAP HELP!!!"

Jason later admitted he had visions of his baby sliding straight out of the tub and launching across the bathroom like a waterpark ride.

Reality check: the baby was slightly startled, but fine. Jason learned to use less bath soap, and now he's a bath time pro.

Lesson? *Small slip-ups don't equal lifetime trauma. You'll keep learning and getting better.*

Good news: Babies are basically tiny, squishy superheroes.

> *"Babies are tougher than they look. If they weren't, humanity wouldn't have made it past the caveman days."*
>
> — Dr. Laura Jana, Pediatrician

Common Mistakes (And How to Avoid Them)

Mistake #1: Comparing yourself to others

Social media is a lie. The dad who looks like he's crushing the 'dad life' on Instagram? His toddler probably ate crayons for breakfast, too.

Mistake #2: Expecting perfection

Perfection is a myth.

Mistake #3: Ignoring your gut instinct

You have dad instincts. They're just... under construction. Trust them.

Mistake #4: Not asking for help

Asking for help is not failure, it's survival.

Real-Life Anecdote

Mark from Seattle was alone with his three-month-old daughter when she started crying non-stop. His mind went blank. He froze, holding her like a ticking time bomb.

His solution? He panicked and sang 'Baby Shark' on loop for ten minutes. Shockingly, it worked. His daughter stopped crying, mostly out of confusion.

Lesson? *When in doubt, sing something ridiculous. Babies are easily confused.*

Signs You're Already a Good Dad? Check

Use this checklist to score yourself from 1–10 (1 = "I need work," 10 = "Dad of the Year"). Add up your points at the end!

Checklist Item	**Your Score (1–10)**
I worry about my baby's well-being.	
I try to be present, even when tired.	
I've learned to survive on no sleep.	
I ask for help when I need it.	
I comfort my baby, even if it doesn't work immediately.	
I clean up disasters (bodily fluids, explosions).	
I laugh at my own parenting fails.	
I take care of my partner too.	
I tell my baby 'I love you' frequently	
I keep showing up, every single day.	
Total Score:	

If you scored more than 50, you're doing just fine, Dad. Actually, even if you didn't, you're still doing fine — you read this far, didn't you?

***Try This Now*!**

Say "I love you" to your baby out loud.

Even if they just stare blankly at you or respond with a mysterious fart noise, you're doing parenting right. Bonus points if you say it while changing a diaper — that's true love.

Closing Thoughts

If you're worried, it means you care. If you care, you're already on your way to being a great dad.

CHAPTER 19

Baby's First Words... Probably Not 'Daddy'

Decoding Baby Babble Without a Translator

"If they don't say 'Dad' first, it's okay. You'll still be their hero."

— Anonymous

Brace yourself, Dad. Despite your relentless efforts (and the hours you've spent whispering *"Da-da"* into your baby's ear like a motivational coach), odds are your little bundle of joy is going to say *"Mama"* first.

Don't take it personally. According to child development experts, babies are more likely to say sounds that come easier to them. "M" is a nasal sound made with closed lips, and since babies love mouthing everything in sight (including their own hands), *"Mama"* often slips out before *"Dada"*.

But here's the good news: *Once they start, it's like popcorn, words pop up everywhere.*

> **Did You Know?**
> *Babies typically say their first real word around 12 months, but they start babbling meaningfully as early as 6 months! (Source: American Speech-Language-Hearing Association)*

Now let's dive into the hilarious, messy, and unforgettable journey of decoding your baby's very first words.

The Beautiful Chaos of Baby Babble

Before you hear that magical first word, you'll go through months of what can best be described as baby gibberish — a charming mix of squeals, grunts, and what sounds like angry complaints to customer service.

Let's be clear: *They're talking. To you. You just don't speak fluent "Baby" yet.*

Real-Life Anecdote

Mike, a first-time dad from Ohio, was convinced his 8-month-old daughter Emily's first word was "guacamole."

"We were at Chipotle, and I swear, clear as day, she looked me dead in the eye and said, 'Guac!'" Mike recalls.

While it's unlikely that Mike's baby was placing her first Mexican food order, what's happening is your baby is experimenting with sounds they hear often. So, if you're the kind of dad who yells "*Touchdown!*" during every game, don't be surprised if your baby's first word sounds suspiciously sporty.

How Babies Learn to Talk:

Babies are natural eavesdroppers. From day one, they're soaking up the rhythm and tone of your voice. But it's not just words they're learning — it's the melody of speech. Babies love high-pitched, sing-song voices.

> ***Did you know?***
> *Studies show that 'parentese' — that high-pitched, exaggerated way of speaking to babies — actually helps with language development! (Source: University of Washington, 2020)*

So go ahead, sing the grocery list. Narrate the weather. Read your baby the back of the shampoo bottle. They're not picky.

> ***Pro Dad Hack:*** *Your baby's favorite radio station is you. Keep the chatter flowing, even when it feels like you're talking to a houseplant.*

Milestones to Watch

Here's a rough guide to what's normal — but remember, *babies love doing things on their own timeline.*

Age	**What to Expect**
3–6 months	Coos, gurgles, and testing out sounds.
6–9 months	Babbling are like mini podcasters: "ba-ba," "da-da," "ga-ga."
9–12 months	First words might appear! Usually familiar things like "mama," "dada," or favorite objects.
12+ months	Two-word phrases start to pop up. Prepare to be amazed (and occasionally confused).

Real-Life Anecdote

Take Sarah and Tom from Texas. They spent months coaching their son Ethan to say "Mama" or "Dada" But no. Ethan's first word?

"I couldn't believe it," Tom said. "We had this whole bet going, and then he grabs the TV remote, points it at the screen, and says, 'Remote'."

Try This Now!

Here's a little homework. Spend a week recording your baby's daily babble sessions.

- *Morning coos? Record.*
- *Post-nap rants? Record.*
- *Suspicious words? Record.*

Not only will you have a priceless audio time capsule, but you'll also start to notice patterns in their sounds. It's like decoding a secret language — except way cuter.

Encouraging Those First Words (Without Desperation)

Even though you can't force your baby to say "Dada," there are a few things you can do to cheer them along:

1. **Talk all day.**
   Narrate life like it's your personal podcast.
   Example: "And now, Daddy attempts to fold laundry while holding a wiggly octopus disguised as a baby!"

2. **Read, read, read.**
   Books expose babies to new words and sounds. Bonus: you'll finally get to use all those silly voices.

3. **Sing.**
   You can give tough competition to Cacofonix (Asterix and Obelix fame), doesn't matter. Singing helps babies learn rhythm and tone.

4. **Play the name game.**
   Point to things and name them. Repetition is your friend: *"Ball! Ball! Look at the ball!"*

Keeping Your Cool When Your Baby Says "Mama" First

You've done the diaper runs at 3 a.m., you've assembled 400-piece playpens with your bare hands, and *still,* your baby looks you in the eye and says, "Mama."

Sure, it stings! Here's how to cope:

- Remind yourself: It's not personal, it's phonetics.
- Use humor: "Fine, I'll just go be the unsung hero in the background."
- Remember: once they start, you'll be hearing "Daaaad!" constantly.

> *"Be careful what you wish for. Once they learn 'Dad,' you'll be summoned 47 times an hour."*
>
> — Every parent ever

Real-Life Anecdote

Jason, a new dad from Florida, thought he was crushing the whole "talk to your baby constantly" advice. Every morning, he'd peel a banana and announce to his 10-month-old daughter Lily:

"Banana time!"

One morning, as Jason reached for the fruit bowl, Lily stretched her arms toward him, locked eyes, and blurted out: *"Nana!"*

Jason dropped the banana!

"I wasn't ready," Jason laughed. "My kid's first word wasn't Dad, wasn't Mom — it was banana. But hey, I'll take it!"

Lesson? *Celebrate the small wins.*

How to React to the First Word

No matter what word your baby blurts out, your job is to react like you just won the lottery!

Pump your fists in the air. Cheer. Call the grandparents. Heck, text your entire contact list if you must.

Why? Because babies love seeing you excited. Your reaction encourages them to keep trying, keep talking, and keep accidentally saying hilarious things that will make for great wedding toasts later in life.

> 💡 ***Pro Dad Hack:*** *Capture the moment on video if you can. The future-you will thank present-you.*

Try This Now!
Take a moment to jot this down:

- *What's the funniest sound your baby has made this week?*
- *What's one new word (or sound) you'd love to hear next?*

When to (Not) Worry

If your baby isn't talking yet, breathe. Every baby hits milestones at their own pace. Some are chatterboxes from day one. Others take their sweet time and suddenly leap from silence to full sentences.

> 💡 ***Did You Know?***
> *Boys, on average, may start talking a bit later than girls — but they catch up quickly! (Source: Mayo Clinic)*

If by 15-18 months your little one isn't saying a few words, chat with your pediatrician for peace of mind. But trust the process — and in the meantime, keep chatting, singing, and narrating life.

The Silent (but Still Talking) Types

Remember, not all communication is verbal. If your baby's waving, clapping, or giving you side-eye when you forget snack time — that's communication.

Celebrate gestures just as much as words. After all, a well-timed look of "Dad, seriously?" is worth a thousand words.

Key Chapter Takeaways

The words will come, till then, patience. Remember:

- First words come at their own pace — and are often surprising.
- Your voice matters. Talk, read, and sing to your baby.
- Don't sweat the "Mama" first. Your time will come, Dad.
- Capture the moments. Record, track, and laugh at every stage.

~

CHAPTER 20

From Goo-Goo to Genius

Helping Your Baby Build Brainpower, Even If You Still Feel Clueless

"The early bird might get the worm, but the curious baby gets the whole encyclopedia (and tries to eat it)."

— Unknown

Picture this: You're staring at your baby, who is drooling on a plastic giraffe with the focus of a chess grandmaster. You, meanwhile, are wondering:

"Am I doing enough to make this tiny human smart?"

Good news: *Your baby is already wired for brilliance.* You don't need to be a neuroscientist to help your baby get there. You just need enthusiasm, patience, and occasionally, the willingness to sing "Old MacDonald" like you're headlining at Madison Square Garden.

This chapter is your dad-friendly guide to unlocking your baby's brainpower — without losing your own in the process.

Understanding Your Baby's Brain

Babies aren't born with 'blank slates'. They're born with about *100 billion neurons* — roughly the same as an adult brain.

> 💡 ***Did You Know?***
> *"By age three, a child's brain has formed about 1,000 trillion connections — about twice as many as adults have!"*
>
> *— Source: Zero to Three Foundation*

Your baby's brain is basically in overdrive, creating and pruning neural pathways at lightning speed. Every smile, cuddle, silly sound, and peekaboo game strengthens those connections.

Dad's Toolbox for Building a Brilliant Brain

Here's where you come in. Don't underestimate the power of your goofy faces and made-up songs. Science says you're making your kid smarter, even if your neighbors think you've lost your mind.

Tool #1: Talk Like You're on a Podcast

Example: "Alright, buddy, we're grabbing the blue onesie today because Dad still can't figure out how to fold the cute striped one."

Studies show babies love the sound of their parents' voices, and the more words they hear, the better their language skills.

> ***Did You Know?***
> *The number of words a child hears in the first three years is strongly linked to their vocabulary and IQ later on.*
>
> — *Hart & Risley Study*

Tool #2: Read Before They Can Read

Start reading now. Yes, even if they chew the pages.

Books with bold pictures and rhythmic language are perfect. Your baby isn't critiquing your reading style, they're soaking up sounds, patterns, and your soothing tone.

Tool #3: Playtime = Brain Time

Tummy time? Brain boost.

Rattles? Brain boost.

Peekaboo? Yep, you guessed it.

Play isn't just fun — it teaches cause and effect, motor skills, and social interactions. So go ahead and build that lopsided block tower with pride.

Tool #4: Music and Movement

Music stimulates both sides of the brain. Dancing (or gentle wiggling) boosts coordination and sensory development. So, pump up those lullabies and make your living room the hottest baby club in town.

> ***Did You Know?***
> *Babies recognize melodies they heard in the womb. If you played 'Bohemian Rhapsody' while your partner was pregnant, congrats: you've got a tiny Queen fan.*
>
> — *University of Helsinki Study, 2013*

Real-Life Anecdote

Greg from Chicago took the "talk to your baby" advice to the next level. He narrated *everything,* including diaper changes ("Wow, we've got a Code Yellow!") and vacuuming ("Now Dad is chasing dust bunnies!").

His wife thought he was losing it — until their baby started babbling after just five months.

💡 Pro Dad Hacks for Boosting Brainpower

Hack #1: Make diaper time learning time

Name their body parts as you clean (bonus: it also distracts them from the chilly wipe).

Hack #2: Face time (not the app)

Babies love looking at faces. So, get close and let them study yours. Make expressions, stick out your tongue, or play mirror games. It's simple and super effective.

Hack #3: Rotate toys

Babies love novelty. Instead of buying new toys every week, rotate the ones you have. It's like giving them a new toy without spending a dime.

Hack #4: Everyday exploration

Take them on 'baby field trips' — walks in the park, trips to the grocery store, even watching the washing machine spin. Narrate what you see and let them soak it in.

Hack #5: Label everything

Point and name objects constantly: "Here's your bottle. That's your pacifier. And this is Dad's coffee — which is very, very important."
Babies build vocabulary way before they can speak.

Hack #6: Baby sign language

Simple signs like "milk," "more," and "all done" can help babies communicate before they can speak. Plus, it feels like your baby is a genius every time they signal "milk" instead of screaming.

Did You Know?

Babies as young as 6 months can start using simple signs, often reducing frustration for both baby and parents.
— Baby Sign Language Research, California State University

Hack #7: Messy play is smart play
Let them squish food, smear paint, and splash water. Sensory play builds brain connections.

Hack #8: Keep it simple (and Repeat)
Repetition builds memory. Don't be shy about reading the same book twelve times in one day. Your baby's brain loves predictability.

"A child's mind is not a container to be filled but rather a fire to be kindled."
— Dorothea Brande

Don't Give Your Baby What It Wants Most: Mobile Phone

The mobile phone is the most popular tool for parents to get their baby to shut up, to eat or to just keep busy in general. Babies simply love the mobile and operate the phone like a pro, making the instruction manual redundant.

Beware.

You won't realise when your baby has turned the tables against you by demanding the phone as a pre-condition to shut up or to eat. Wait there's more.

Studies show that *heavy phone use can impair a child's ability to develop emotional intelligence and form healthy relationships*. In fact, The American Academy of Pediatrics recommends *avoiding screens for babies under 18 months* (except for video chatting with Grandma).

💡***Pro Dad Hack:*** *If you want to limit screen time for your baby, apply this rule to yourself first. Babies have this habit of mimicking their parents.*

Try This Now!

Rate your current brain-building efforts. Score each parameter from 1 (What's that?) to 10 (Nailed it!).

Activity	***Your Score (1–10)***
Talking to your baby daily	
Reading books, even if chewed	
Playtime with simple toys	
Dance parties / music time	
Daily tummy time	
Face time (real, not virtual)	
Narrating your day	
Rotating toys for novelty	

Total your score:

- ***70–80:*** *You're doing awesome! Keep up the good work.*
- ***50–69:*** *Good going, you can do better!*
- ***Below 50:*** *Rookie Brain Builder (Don't worry — there's always tomorrow!)*

Closing Thoughts

Your baby's brain is growing faster than you can say "developmental milestone," and you're doing a fantastic job of feeding it with love, laughter, and learning.

~

CHAPTER 21

Fatherhood: The Job with No Lunch Breaks

Why Parenting is The Ultimate 'Forever Project'

> *"Being a dad is the only job where success means getting fired—because one day, they won't need you anymore."*
>
> — Unknown

Welcome to the Job You Can't Quit

Congratulations, my friend. You've officially accepted the position of 'Dad', a full-time, non-stop, lifetime contract with zero lunch breaks, no sick days, and the wildest assortment of responsibilities known to mankind. Some days, you're the personal butler to a tiny overlord. Other days, you're the chief giggle officer. And once in a while, you're a human napkin.

Here's the twist: *you're never getting promoted.*

No corner office. No gold watch. But there's an upside! Every laugh, hug, "I love you, Dad," and drooly smile is worth a thousand pay checks.

> ***Did You Know?***
> *According to a Pew Research Center study, 63% of dads say being a father is "extremely important to their identity."*

The Long-Term Impact of Fatherhood

Right now, it feels like you're stuck in an endless cycle of diaper changes, midnight wake-up calls, and coffee consumption that could frighten a Starbucks barista. But you're not just surviving — you're shaping a life.

You're planting seeds

Think of fatherhood like gardening (minus the fertilisers and pesticides). You plant seeds every time you read Goodnight Moon for the thousandth time. You water them with bedtime kisses and goofy jokes at breakfast. Someday, those seeds grow into confident, kind, fully functioning humans.

Sure, it might not feel magical when you're scrubbing off scribbled writing off the wall, but you're building something extraordinary.

The invisible ROI

You won't see the results immediately. There's no quarterly performance review where your baby evaluates your snuggling efficiency. But one day, your kid will do something awesome — like hold the door open for someone or share their last gummy bear — and you'll think, *Hey, I had something to do with that!*

The Hard Moments Are Worth It

There will be days — oh, so many days — when you wonder: *Is this worth it?*

Like when you've changed the fifth diaper explosion of the morning, or when you step on a toy xylophone at 3:00 a.m. and discover new curse words in your brain.

The answer is yes.

Why? Because the exhausting, soul-draining moments are building resilience. In you *and* your child.

As motivational speaker Jim Rohn once said: *"It's not what you get from achieving your goals, it's who you become."*

You're becoming the dad your kid will remember forever. And no one remembers the clean floors or perfectly balanced lunches. They remember the giggles, the shoulder rides, and the time you heroically saved Mr. Teddy from the washing machine.

Common Dad Traps: Comparing Progress

Here's the thing. Parenting isn't a race. Yet, we dads love to compare:

- "Does my baby roll over fast enough?"
- "Why does their kid sleep through the night and mine parties at 2 a.m.?"
- "That dad built a treehouse. I can't even assemble IKEA furniture without a meltdown."

Relax! Every kid is different, and so is every dad.

Did You Know?

The average baby starts crawling between 6 to 10 months, but some skip crawling altogether and go straight to walking. No one's handing out trophies for "Fastest Crawl Time."

Your job isn't to match someone else's highlight reel. It's to enjoy *your* family's blooper reel.

The Forever Project: Embrace the Journey

Here's the part no one warns you about.

Parenting never really ends. Even when they move out, even when they have kids of their own, you'll still be "Dad."

And that's beautiful. You're not raising a baby, you're raising an adult.

You're the voice in their head reminding them to wear a jacket when it's cold. You're the reason they'll know how to change a tire or apologize when they mess up.

Try This Now!

Find an old photo — one with you in a diaper, hair sticking up like a baby porcupine, probably crying because your bottle was empty.

Now think: Your parents survived you.

They had the same doubts, fears, and "What in the world am I doing?" moments. And yet, here you are. Fully grown. Functioning (mostly). Capable of keeping a small human alive.

If they could do it, so can you.

Real-Life Anecdote

Matt wanted to surprise his toddler with a special pancake breakfast. He found a recipe online titled 'Easy, Foolproof Pancakes'.

Actually, there was nothing foolproof about it.

Matt accidentally quadrupled the baking powder, creating pancake batter that resembled expanding foam insulation. When he poured it onto the griddle, the batter exploded into a fluffy monster that oozed over the sides like volcanic lava.

His toddler thought it was *hilarious*. "Daddy made pancake aliens!" she squealed.

Matt considered it a disaster. His wife considered ordering waffles from a diner. But their daughter? She declared it the best breakfast ever.

Lesson? *Aim for progress, not perfection. Sometimes, pancake aliens are the highlight of the day.*

When to Actually Feel Bad?

Short answer? *Never.* Stop feeling guilty.

Missed bedtime because of work? It happens. Accidentally got distracted and let the pacifier fall on the dog bed? Relax. (Just rinse it.) Forgot it was pyjama day at daycare? Laugh it off.

The only times you should really feel bad are:

- **Actual neglect.** (Which, if you're reading this, is not you.)
- **Not trying at all.** (Again, if you're reading this, is not you.)
- **Refusing to let yourself enjoy the journey.**

Everything else? *Forgive yourself.*

~

Closing Thoughts

Welcome to the Dad Club: Lifetime Membership Included

> *"Being a dad means showing up, messing up, cleaning up, and loving every second of it."*
>
> — Anonymous

At the end of the day, this job isn't about perfection. It's about your presence and showing up every day.

Your kid doesn't care if you can build a Pinterest-worthy nursery. They care if you're there to read a bedtime story (even if you accidentally skip a page and they call you out).

Celebrate the small wins:

- The first time your baby grabs your finger.
- The first giggle.
- The first sticky, peanut-butter-covered hug.

These moments *are* the paycheck.

And remember, being a dad might not come with lunch breaks, but it comes with something way better — a lifetime of love, laughs, and memories you'll treasure forever.

Now go high-five yourself in the mirror, and get ready for tomorrow's adventure.

BONUS CHAPTER

FAQs Every First-Time Dad Secretly Has (But Doesn't Always Ask)

1. **How often should I feed my newborn?**
   Newborns need to be fed every 2 - 3 hours, which translates to 8 to 12 times in a 24-hour period. Yes, even at 3:17 a.m.

2. **Why does my baby keep falling asleep while feeding?**
   It's normal. Feeding is comforting and tiring for babies. If they keep dozing off early, try gently waking them by tickling their feet or changing their diaper.

3. **How do I know if my baby is getting enough milk?**
   Look for steady weight gain, regular wet diapers (at least 6 a day), and a generally satisfied baby post-feed. Trust the pee and poop math.

4. **What should I do if my baby hasn't pooped in 24 hours?**
   It depends on age. In the first few weeks, daily poops are expected. After that, fewer are okay if the baby seems happy and feeds well. If you're worried, call the pediatrician.

5. **What causes diaper rash and how do I treat it?**
   Wetness, friction, or leftover poop can cause it. Keep the area clean and dry, change diapers frequently, and use a good zinc oxide diaper cream.

If the diaper rash stays for 3-4 days or turns into a sore that won't go away or spreads, consult a pediatrician.

6. **How do I bathe a newborn safely?**
Start with sponge baths until the umbilical cord falls off. Use lukewarm water, support the head and neck.

7. **When will the umbilical cord stump fall off?**
Usually within 1 to 2 weeks. Don't pull it off, even if it looks like it's hanging by a thread. It's not a Lego piece.

8. **Why does my baby cry so much?**
Crying is their way of communicating. They may be hungry, gassy, tired, overstimulated, or just want to be held. Sometimes, they cry for reasons only they understand.

9. **Why does my baby sleep all day and stay awake all night?**
Their internal clock is still set to womb-time. It takes a few weeks (or more) for their circadian rhythm to figure out Earth's time zones.

10. **Do newborns need a strict sleep schedule?**
Not really. Follow their cues and aim for patterns, not perfection. A basic routine helps, but don't expect consistency just yet.

11. **What temperature is considered a fever in a newborn?**
Anything above 100.4°F (38°C). Call your pediatrician immediately if your baby is under 3 months old and runs a fever.

12. **When should my baby get their vaccinations?**
Start planning for vaccinations before your baby is born. Your pediatrician will guide you, but the first round usually happens around 6–8 weeks. Yes, they'll cry. So will you. But it's important.

Note: Most public schools require vaccine records.

13. **When should I start tummy time[1]?**
As early as the first week—just a few minutes a day as long as they're awake and supervised. It helps strengthen neck and shoulder muscles. It's also helpful for moving baby gas.

Note: Don't do tummy time after eating or burping, it creates a mess!

14. **Is it ok to carry my baby in a baby carrier right away?**
Only if it supports their head and neck well. Check the age and weight recommendations. And read the manual—seriously.

15. **Is it safe for my baby to sleep in a swing or car seat?**
Not for long naps or overnight sleep. Always place your baby on a flat, firm surface to sleep. Swings are for awake time.

16. **Will rocking my baby to sleep become a bad habit?**
Only if you consider closeness and comfort a bad thing. Many parents rock their babies to sleep—it's fine. You can always adjust later.

17. **Can I give water to my baby?**
Not before 6 months. Their tiny tummies are made for milk—breastmilk or formula only, please.

18. **When can I introduce solid foods?**
Usually around 6 months, but talk to your pediatrician first. And start with simple, single-ingredient options.

19. **Why does my baby's skin look dry or flaky?**
Newborn skin can peel in the early weeks. Use a mild, fragrance-free moisturizer. If it looks red, itchy, or cracked, check with your doctor.

1 Tummy time is laying babies on their stomachs for brief periods while they're awake.

20. **Is it safe to sleep in the same bed as my baby?**
Experts recommend room-sharing, not bed-sharing. A separate bassinet next to your bed is safest.

21. **Can my partner still breastfeed if she has mastitis?**
Yes—and it's actually encouraged. Continued breastfeeding can help clear blocked ducts. Support your partner (and maybe bring snacks).

22. **Does what the breastfeeding parent eats affect the baby?**
Yes, flavours can pass through milk. If baby seems unusually fussy after a meal, consider eliminating certain foods one at a time.

23. **Should I wipe every time my baby pees?**
Yes. Gentle cleaning prevents rashes and infections. Wet wipes or a soft cloth work fine. *Bonus tip: wait a second after opening the diaper—surprise pee is real.*

24. **Why do I feel overwhelmed even though I love my baby?**
Because this is hard. And messy. And nonstop. You're not alone—talk to your partner, friends, or a counsellor if needed. Taking care of yourself helps you take better care of your baby.

25. **Why does my baby grunt, snort, or sound like a tiny farm animal while sleeping?**
Newborns are noisy sleepers. It's often due to immature nasal passages and digestion. Unless they seem distressed, it's perfectly normal. Sleep with earplugs, not panic.

26. **Is it okay if I don't feel instantly connected to my baby?**
Yes, that's more common than you think. Bonding takes time, especially when you're running on zero sleep and burp cloths. Be present, stay patient—it will come.

27. **How do I burp a baby who refuses to burp?**
Try switching positions: over the shoulder, sitting upright, or on

your lap face-down. Gently rub or pat the back. Or just wait—sometimes they burp on their own... or the other end takes over.

28. **Why does my baby cry the moment I sit down?**
Babies have highly sensitive anti-sitting radar. Try walking, swaying, or bouncing. Sitting down is suspicious. Standing = trustworthy.

29. **Can I take my newborn outside?**
Yes, fresh air is good for both of you. Just keep baby shaded, dressed appropriately, and away from crowds. Think 'neighborhood stroll',not 'music festival.'

30. **What's the best way to soothe a baby during a meltdown?**
Try the "5 S's": swaddle, side/stomach position, shush, swing, and suck (pacifier or feeding). They don't always work in order—but experiment and find your combo.

31. **How do I keep my relationship strong while adjusting to parenthood?**
Communicate. Divide baby duties. Make time for each other (even if it's just watching a show between diaper changes). And say thank you often—it goes a long way.

32. **What if I make a mistake?**
You will. Everyone does. The goal isn't perfection—it's being present, learning, and doing your best. Apologize when needed, and keep showing up.

33. **Do I really need all this baby gear?**
Nope. Some of it's great, some of it's marketing. Focus on the basics—safe sleep space, feeding tools, diapers, wipes, and love. Everything else is negotiable.

A Special Request For You

If you made it this far, first of all—high five! Thank you so much for taking the time to read this book!

Did you enjoy the book and get valuable insights? If this book made you laugh, helped you feel less clueless, or just gave you a little boost on your wild dad journey...

👉 **Could you please take a moment to leave a 5-star review on Amazon.com?**

It takes less than a minute, costs nothing, but it means the world to me—and helps more confused, anxious, awesome first-time dads find this guide (and keeps me motivated to keep writing through the chaos).

Your words matter more than you know.

Simply click the link below or scan the QR code to share your review and make a big difference in someone's life.

https://www.amazon.com/review/review-your-purchases/?asin=BOOKASIN

Thank you for being part of this hilarious, messy, beautiful ride.

With diapers and gratitude,

Caleb Darnell

Sources

- *Breastfeeding vs. Formula Feeding.* (n.d.). Mount Sinai Health System. https://www.mountsinai.org/health-library/special-topic/breastfeeding-vs-formula-feeding
- *Breastfeeding vs. Formula Feeding (for Parents).* (n.d.). https://kidshealth.org/en/parents/breast-bottle-feeding.html
- Crider, C. (2019, December 19). *What is controlled crying and will it help your baby sleep?* Healthline. https://www.healthline.com/health/baby/controlled-crying#what-it-is
- Twenge, J. M., Haidt, J., Twenge, J. M., Giedd, J. N., Brown, V. A., & Dunckley, V. L. (n.d.). How early use of cell phones affects brain development. In *Sources.* https://www.hamilton.k12.wi.us/wp-content/uploads/2024/10/Brain-develpment-and-cell-phones.pdf#:~:text=Delayed%20Maturation:%20The%20prefrontal%20cortex%2C%20which%20governs,and%20games%2C%20can%20interfere%20with%20the%20natural
- Sleep Junkie
  New Parent Sleep Loss Statistics. Sleep Junkie, 2020.
  Retrieved from: https://www.sleepjunkie.com/sleep-loss-new-parents/
- Williamson, A., & Feyer, A.-M.
  Moderate sleep deprivation produces impairments in cognitive and motor performance equivalent to legally prescribed levels of alcohol intoxication. Occupational & Environmental Medicine, vol. 57, no. 10, 2000, pp. 649–655.
  DOI: 10.1136/oem.57.10.649
- National Sleep Foundation.
  Parental Sleep Deprivation. SleepFoundation.org, 2021.
  Retrieved from: https://www.sleepfoundation.org/parental-sleep-deprivation
- Moonkie. (2024, March 14). 25 questions first-time parents ask about their newborn. *Moonkie.* https://moonkieshop.com/blogs/news/first-time-parents-questions?srsltid=AfmBOordFglIRWQOh0LKEkwldI-OlopWS5jkSOQLtoghoqcQh3GGZF_-

- Harris, N. (2024, September 23). *The ultimate guide to baby poop colors.* Parents. https://www.parents.com/baby/diapers/dirty/baby-poop-guide/
- Bishop, K. (2023, May 17). *How Kids Change Your Relationship Part 1 | Kim & Rog.* Kim & Rog. https://kimandrog.com/how-kids-change-your-relationship-part-1/
- *What is sleep training?* (2021, February 2). Baby Merlin's Magic Sleepsuit. https://www.magicsleepsuit.com/blogs/mss-blog/what-is-sleep-training
- A baby carrier for your baby? No, more for mom and dad! (2024, April 26). *ROOKIE.* https://rookie-baby.eu/blogs/news/a-baby-carrier-for-your-baby-no-more-for-mom-and-dad
- Spencer, J. A., Moran, D. J., Lee, A., & Talbert, D. (1990). White noise and sleep induction. *Archives of Disease in Childhood,* 65(1), 135–137.
- HealthyChildren.org (American Academy of Pediatrics). *What's in Your Baby's Diaper?*
  https://www.healthychildren.org
  → Used for definitions of normal vs. abnormal poop colors, including yellow, brown, green, and white.
- Seattle Children's Hospital. *Poop – Unusual Colors* (Health Advice)
  https://www.seattlechildrens.org
  → Source for understanding when stool colors (like red, white, black, or gray) may require medical attention.
- Mayo Clinic. *Baby poop: What's normal?* https://www.mayoclinic.org
  → Used for general reference on frequency, texture, and color of infant stool during various developmental stages.
- National Institute of Diabetes and Digestive and Kidney Diseases (NIDDK). *Symptoms & Causes of Biliary Atresia.* https://www.niddk.nih.gov
  → Referenced for explanation of white or gray poop as a sign of possible liver/bile duct issues.
- Nemours KidsHealth. *What's That in the Diaper? A Quick Guide to Baby Poop* https://kidshealth.org → Supported the interpretation of meconium, orange, green, and blue stools in infants.
- Source of images: ChatGPT

www.ingramcontent.com/pod-product-compliance
Lightning Source LLC
Chambersburg PA
CBHW062140160726
48282CB00027B/884
* 9 7 8 8 1 9 5 5 9 8 4 9 6 *